DISRUPTING BURNOUT

The Professional Woman's Lifeline to Finding Purpose

Dr. Patrice Buckner Jackson

Disclaimers

Although the publisher and the author have made every effort to ensure that the information in this book was correct at press time and while this publication is designed to provide accurate information in regard to the subject matter covered, the publisher and the author assume no responsibility for errors, inaccuracies, omissions, or any other inconsistencies herein and hereby disclaim any liability to any party for any loss, damage, or disruption caused by errors or omissions, whether such errors or omissions result from negligence, accident, or any other cause.

The information presented is the author's opinion and does not constitute any health or medical advice. The content of this book is for informational purposes only and is not intended to diagnose, treat, cure, or prevent any condition or disease.

Please seek advice from your healthcare provider for your personal health concerns prior to taking healthcare advice from this book.

The publisher and the author make no guarantees concerning the level of success you may experience by following the advice and strategies contained in this book, and you accept the risk that results will differ for each individual. The testimonials and examples provided in this book show exceptional results, which may not apply to the average reader, and are not intended to represent or guarantee that you will achieve the same or similar results.

Any internet addresses, phone numbers, or company or product information printed in this book are offered as a resource and are not intended in any way to be or imply an endorsement by, the publisher or the author nor does the publisher or author vouch for the existence, content, or services of these sites, phone numbers, companies, or products beyond the life of this book.

Some names and identifying information have been changed to protect the privacy of clients.

To the woman with the heavy load,

I see you.

This is for you.

Contents

There's a Name for That

You're an accomplished woman with many responsibilities, and you often find yourself overwhelmed, exhausted, and burned out. I know. I've been there. As a matter of fact, burnout almost cost me everything. You're reading this book because everyone recognizes and desires your gifts, but they have no idea what it costs to be you. You give so much to others that you have very little left for yourself. You work with your empathy meter on high most days, and it is exhausting. You often find yourself depleted after serving others, and you feel your efforts are taken for granted. You feel misused by everyone in your life, including those who love you. You feel guilty because everyone around you thinks you've got it all together. If they only knew.

People tell you to put it all in God's hands, but no one taught you how to do that. There's no margin in your life; you could literally be doing something for someone every minute of every day if your body could handle it. You run to isolation just to catch your breath. However, you don't find this escape refreshing. You've been very successful in your professional life, but if you are honest, you know you're still searching for purpose.

You struggle with perfectionism, holding yourself to a higher standard than you hold others. You also struggle with comparison, never feeling like enough as you compare yourself to other professional women with clean houses, perfect partners, extraordinary children, and a laundry list of professional accolades. You may even find the work you once loved is now wearing you thin, which distresses your soul. Now you're questioning if you were truly called to do this work in the first place. You're career frustrated. You feel checked out and no longer interested in things you once loved. Your emotions are all over the place and your wellness habits seem to have vanished from your life. You taught everyone in your life that you could be all things to all people, and they believed you. Now, Friend, you just want to run away from it all. You think you are all alone. You feel like the only successful woman living with these struggles. Friend, it's not just you. You did not make this up. There's a name for all of that. It's called *burnout*. More specifically, I call this the Cycle of Burnout, but we'll discuss that in detail in chapter 3.

Hi, Friend!

I'm Dr. Patrice Buckner Jackson, but you can call me PBJ. All my friends do. I call you "Friend" because we have some things in common. I am a wife, a Mama Patrice (i.e., a stepmama), a daughter, a big sister, an aunt, a mentor, a friend, a minister, a transformational speaker, an educator for almost twenty-five years now, an executive coach, and now, an author. Honestly, there aren't many professional goals I set for myself that I haven't attained, and at each accomplishment, I felt like I needed the next one—the next promotion, the next project, or the next accolade. I expected the next one to bring the peace I longed to experience. I was searching for a finish line, but I only found more curves and detours. I brought all of myself to everything I did, and I lost myself.

In this book, you will learn three proven strategies for disrupting burnout so you can discover your innate, unique brilliance. For now, know that you will release mindsets that keep you trapped in the Cycle of Burnout and you'll create new belief systems that accelerate your true brilliance. This is more than self-care. This is about recovery and revival.

I'll share my own testimony, share testimonies from my clients, and teach you, step by step, the strategies we use to beat burnout. Please note: Clients' names and identifying details have been changed throughout this book to protect the integrity of their journey. These stories are shared to allow you to see what is possible, but remember every journey is unique. Your journey will not mirror any story shared here. Your journey is specifically crafted to you alone.

Throughout this book, I will encourage you to seek the services of a licensed counselor as this book is not intended to be a substitute for therapy. I encourage all my clients to work with a counselor as they implement the strategies discussed here to ensure they have the support necessary to accomplish deep work.

Friend, it's time for you to get your breath back. Take this journey out of burnout and into brilliance with me.

Chapter 1

I Was Born for This

As dean of students at a university, part of my job was to respond to and manage student crises. However, no professional development workshop, graduate course, or textbook could have prepared me for the tragedy we faced on that April day in 2015. My day was dedicated to meeting with a group of students protesting in the president's office. Everyone on my team knew these students were my priority of the day. I'd set aside several hours to prepare for them, meet with them, and listen to them. My staff knew to hold calls and triage all other concerns so I could focus on those students. I sincerely desired to support them and facilitate communication between them and university administration.

We gathered in a conference room down the hall from my office suite to have some separation from the flow of the office. As the students shared their concerns, my executive assistant came to the glass door and motioned for me to come out. I must admit I was a bit frustrated. *What in the world could be more important than this?* I asked the students to excuse me, and disdain colored their faces as I made my way to the hall.

My assistant started with an apology. Then she explained, "Chief called. She needs you at university police right now."

"Did she say what she needed?"

"No, ma'am. She just said you need to come right now."

I took a deep breath and walked back into the conference room. "I am so sorry. I set aside my day for you all, but something has come up. I have to go, but Miss Kim will get you all rescheduled on my calendar as soon as possible. Please know I wouldn't leave if I didn't absolutely have to."

I gathered my things and headed over to the university police department. As soon as I entered the building, I was ushered to a back conference room filled, wall to wall, with police officials. Some were from our campus police department and others from different agencies. Some talked on their phones while others held conversations in small groups. I had no idea what was happening, but I felt it was going to be a bad day. I found a seat and waited for the chief.

She eventually came over with a list of names. "I need you to find out if these people were in class today." I could feel this was no time to ask questions, so I took the list and got to work. I pulled up our information system, accessed class schedules and phone numbers, and started calling professors to inquire about their attendance records for the day. Some hesitated to share without more information about why I needed to know. Others seemed to have an idea something was going on and shared freely. I kept calling until I got enough information for the chief. It wasn't long before I put the context clues together. This day wasn't just bad. It was tragic.

We needed more space and we needed to be close to the impact of the tragedy, so we eventually moved the whole operation to our school of nursing. Seven nursing students had been involved in a deadly car crash on their way to their last day of clinicals. Five students died that day. Two were critically injured, and we didn't know if they would make it. I went from helping the police make positive identifications to working with our communications team to determine how in the world we were going to share this news with our university community.

One of the most difficult moments of the day was breaking the news to a father over the phone. Word had begun to spread and something in his heart knew his child was involved. He called the university several times, but no one could give him an update until we were sure. The moment we had a positive ID, the chief gave me permission to call him.

"Sir, I'm Dr. Patrice Jackson, dean of students at the university. It sounds like you're driving. Can you pull over for a moment?" I waited until I was sure he had stopped. "What is your daughter's name?" I held my breath until he responded. "What's her birth-date?" I closed my eyes. "Sir, I'm so sorry."

After spending some time on the phone with the student's father and getting a family member to meet him on the road, I moved to a large auditorium classroom where two hundred nursing students and their faculty members sat waiting for details. My voice quivered, and my friend, the director of counseling on campus, held my hand as I read the names of the five students who had died and the two who were injured. Sobs and gasps and shrieks filled the room.

There wasn't much more to say at that moment. Sometimes we just need to hold space with people. In times like these, words are inadequate, so you just sit. Your presence is all you can give. It's not enough. Nothing is enough, but presence is something. It is significant.

I couldn't stay in that space long because, by this time, news crews were showing up on our campus. I was ushered from that room to an area where the cameras were set up. I was assigned to speak on behalf of the university. On my way to meet the cameras, I walked past our university president, who had been with us all day. He demonstrated an example of true leadership that day. He was there, but he didn't take over. He made space for each of us to do our work. He trusted our experience. He supported us and stayed close in case we needed him. He was there. I will always be grateful for that.

On my way to meet the news reporters, our president gently grabbed my arm and said, "Patrice, thank you."

Without hesitation, I said, "Sir, I was born for this."

I didn't have time to think about my response. I just kept moving. We went from the news interviews to Greek Row because each of the women who died that day was a member of a different sorority. My colleagues and I visited all five houses just to hold space with those women. Friends gathered on the street and surrounded the women's significant others on the front lawns. Roommates, siblings, and parents gathered on campus. It was the worst day of my entire career.

There was much to do in the days following the tragedy. Honestly, we continued to support students, parents, siblings, and the community for months and years to come. When I reflect on that day, as I do often, I think about my response to the president: "Sir, I was born for this." Where did that come from? Why did that response come out of me? I know it was pure because I had nothing else to offer that day but truth. No one wants to face such a day. No one desires to be there, but somehow, I knew I was supposed to be there.

After fighting through burnout and supporting other women through it, I understand my response so much better now. In that moment, my heart had identified something my mind was not aware of yet. My heart knew I was made for crises. It's my thing. It's what I do well. It's what I have always done. It's what I was born for. Crisis is my shine. It's my light. Crisis is my brilliance. I have an innate, unique brilliance for connecting with people who are struggling and helping them find the light again. When I look back over my life, this is something I have always done, from childhood to this very day. I am the person you call when your life is falling apart. I am the person you call when you cannot see your way through. I am the person you call when you don't know what else to do.

The constant struggle to find my place in the world led me to rock-bottom burnout, but discovering my brilliance freed me to live in power and impact without performing.

Although my brilliance positions me to be exposed to and involved in some tough situations, I have never felt more alive. Standing securely in my brilliance ended a lifelong search for significance. Without a keen awareness of my brilliance, I spiraled into low self-esteem, imposter syndrome, overworking, overwhelm, and burnout. Obtaining the highest degree did not fill the void. Being promoted to the highest position left me lacking. Even having my gifts recognized in church was not enough. The constant struggle to find my place in the world led me to rock-bottom burnout, but discovering my brilliance freed me to live in power and impact without performing.

Friend, there is no replacement for you and the brilliance you were created to pour into the world. No other person can fill your specific shoes. In discovering your brilliance, you will unlock supernatural treasure that blesses the world and fulfills your deepest longing for identity.

There's Treasure in You

If you're wondering if you have brilliance, the answer is yes. Every living, breathing human being is assigned to this earth with a gift from God. You are here on purpose and for purpose. There is no life without God, so regardless of the circumstances of your birth, you're supposed to be here, and you have a treasure inside you. The Apostle Paul taught the church at Ephesus, "For we are God's handiwork, created in Christ Jesus to do good works, which God prepared in advance for us to do" (Ephesians 2:10 [NIV]). This verse proves God created us as His masterpiece to do work He already had in mind. He had plans for you before you took your first breath, Friend.

Paul continues to teach in 2 Corinthians 4:7: "We now have this light shining in our hearts, but we ourselves are like fragile clay jars containing this great treasure. This makes it clear that our great power is from God, not from ourselves." I love the way this verse illuminates the fact that we are all like clay jars, made of dirt, fragile, and not worth much without the light of God that shines through us. He is the treasure within. Through His Spirit each of us carries a specific brilliance that illuminates the world around us. He made us with His very hands to carry His light on the earth. Each of us has a piece of Him that the world needs to experience. There's treasure in you, Friend.

Your treasure is that innate, unique brilliance you were created to bring to the world. Every person has it. Some people call this your purpose. Your purpose is your brilliance, and when you move in purpose, you share that brilliance with the world. Becoming aware of your innate, unique, specific brilliance is the most powerful catalyst of transformation. Discovering my God-given, one-of-a-kind purpose freed me to be me.

Much of my burnout experience was tied to people pleasing, trying to be all things to all people. I no longer contort myself to fit into boxes and definitions created by other people. Discovering my brilliance allows me to show up in wholeness and healing. I focus less on what I do and more on who I am. I accept I am a human being, not a human doing. Focusing on my being increases my impact on the world around me. My heart is free, my mind is clear, and my power has increased. I'm here for a reason and I know what I'm here to do.

Did you know you are brilliant? No, really, Friend, I need you to hear me. You are absolutely brilliant. How do I know? You were created by a brilliant God, and that brilliant God made you in His own image (Genesis 1:27). During her Permission Nights Tour at Forward City Church in Columbia, South Carolina, Dr. Jackie Greene, author of *Permission to Live Free,* shared that we must begin to see ourselves as God is. We often identify what we believe we are not. Dr. Jackie shared, "Many people say, I am not creative, but if God is creative, you are creative." You were made in His image and His Spirit lives in you. If He is strong, you are strong. If He is resourceful, you are as well. If He is brilliant, so are you. If He made the birds of the air and the flowers of the field brilliantly, how much more did He pour into you (Matthew 6:26-34)? You are His masterpiece shaped to look like Him and to be like Him

Purpose Is Brilliance

Your purpose is not your job title or job description. You do not need to wait until you get to a certain level in life to identify your purpose. Purpose is not about recognition, accolades, or promotions. Your purpose is brilliance. It is the genius on the inside of you. Your purpose is the innate, unique brilliance you bring to the world.

Your brilliance is innate. You can't earn it and you didn't learn it. Your brilliance is specifically given to you by God. It's God expressed through you on the earth. This brilliance has been with you for your entire life. Brilliance is in you, even if you can't quite see it yet. Brilliance comes through you every day because you can't help it. Brilliance flows from you without you giving thought to it. It is your gift. It is your thing. It is your shine. It is your purpose.

Something beautiful happens as you do this work. You begin to emerge wholly as the woman God created you to be. In that space, your brilliance is undeniable. Where it used to seep out of you when you were cluttered, brilliance pours from you as you step into freedom. Your purpose will shine forth as you allow God to heal your heart and set you free. The brilliance will be undeniable; you will see yourself as the woman God specifically designed for a specific work on the earth. The light of God's glory will shine forth in such a brilliant way that everyone in your path will be impacted. Your brilliance is freely given to you by your Creator in heaven. It is your spiritual DNA. Brilliance is the way you look like the Father and share His love in the world.

Your brilliance is unique. There is no other just like yours. The same God who numbered the very hairs of your head also created you with a unique, specific gift unlike anyone else's (Luke 12:7). Yannik McKie, pastor of Chosen Church and CEO of Purpose-Fueled Leader, teaches we all have a "purpose print". According to Yannik, just like your fingerprint is unlike any other person's, your purpose print is unique to you alone. You may do similar work, but you will never do it just like another person.

There are thousands of gifted singers in the world, but no one will be Whitney Houston ever again. This isn't just about her sound, but more importantly, it's about the impact she made on our hearts as she flowed in her gift. You may be a teacher, but the impact of your teaching is different. You may be a minister, but the impact of your ministry is unlike anyone else's even if you serve the same demographic of people. No matter what you do to serve, no one else will have the exact impact you have. Your brilliance is holy.

In I Peter 1:16, believers are reminded that we are to be holy as God is holy. The original Greek term for "holy" in this verse is *agios*,[1] which means set apart, revered, sacred, and worthy of veneration. Holy means to be other or unique. Your brilliance is sacred. Your brilliance is like no other. This is why it's so important for you to discover your brilliance. No one else in the world can bring forth your specific gift like you can. The world needs you to be fully you. There is no adequate alternative. You are the one, Sis.

It's Your Superpower and Your Kryptonite

My husband, Edward, is a fan of comic book heroes. He and our daughter enjoy following the journeys of superhuman characters who always somehow save the world. I am not a fan, but I can't help but be exposed to these stories in my house. As I consider your brilliance, my mind goes to the storyline of the X-Men franchise, created by Stan Lee. In this story, Professor Charles Xavier leads an academy of young superheroes who got their powers through different genetic mutations. The goal of the academy is to teach the young mutants how to manage their powers. Without the training, they would be ineffective at the least and destructive at their worst. However, with the wisdom of Professor X, a mutant himself, this team of flawed supernatural beings navigate balancing the power of their gifts with the challenges that come from being extraordinarily gifted. They learn to live in the duality of possessing brilliance.

The same lesson is imperative for you. Your brilliance is your greatest strength and your greatest stumbling block. It is the thing that sets you apart and the thing that can rip you apart if you're not careful to allow God to be your guide. It is your superpower and your kryptonite. In *The Amazing Weight*, author and preacher Marissa Farrow describes this duality of being called to greatness. She shares how just as the miracle of motherhood comes with the "pain of the push," your mission comes with great joy and great trial.[2] Your brilliance can bring freedom to others and bondage to you if you are not careful.

My brilliance of supporting others through their crisis also created my great fall to burnout. I am anointed to support people through their trials, and I must have boundaries in my life to ensure I do not overextend myself for the sake of others. You have a unique brilliance that impacts the world around you, and that same brilliance has a shadow side that can produce negative results for you if you are not submitted and obedient to God.

Keep your brilliance in check by remembering its source. God is your source. Everything else is a resource. Brilliance comes from Him and must be maintained through Him. The brilliance you carry is so magnificent that it cannot be sustained through human logic. It is so powerful that you yourself could be consumed by it if you do not allow God to manage it. He will tell you who, how, and when to serve. He will assign passions and remove them as He sees fit. He will tell you to do a certain work in one season and to leave that same work in a different season.

God created you for your brilliance and He knows how to manage it well. The only way to consistently show up in your brilliance is to continually return to Him for refreshing and refueling. He will manage this massive gift if you submit it back to Him. Trust God to guide, direct, and instruct you in how to use your brilliance so it remains a blessing to others and to you. I'll show you exactly what that looks like in my life and how you can do it.

He Said What He said!

God gifted you before you decided to love Him. He gave you brilliance before you gave Him your heart. Growing up in church, I often heard church folk say, "The gifts of God are without repentance," a paraphrase of Romans 11:29. It took some personal study for me to understand this verse. In the New Living Translation, the verse reads, "For God's gifts and his call can never be withdrawn." In this passage, the Apostle Paul explained that the people of Israel will always be God's chosen people, even when they do not believe in Jesus. God's promise to their ancestors does not change based on their decisions, beliefs, or behavior.

In the same way, the brilliance God placed inside you is yours, and it is powerful whether you believe in Him or not. This point is further supported by the Prophet Jeremiah in Jeremiah 1:5, where he proclaimed on behalf of God "I knew you before I formed you in your mother's womb. Before you were born I set you apart and appointed you as my prophet to the nations." God did not wait to see who we would be or what behavior we would choose once here on earth. He made His mind up about us before we could choose any action. He decided to love you and to believe in you before you could perform, impress, or achieve anything.

Every moment of your life was planned with care. According to Psalm 139:13-18,

> You made all the delicate, inner parts of my body and knit me together in my mother's womb. Thank you for making me so wonderfully complex! Your workmanship is marvelous—how well I know it. You watched me as I was being formed in utter seclusion, as I was woven together in the dark of the womb. You saw me before I was born. Every day of my life was recorded in your book. Every moment was laid out before a single day had passed.
>
> How precious are your thoughts about me, O God. They cannot be numbered! I can't even count them; they

outnumber the grains of sand! And when I wake up, you are still with me!

To put it in today's language, "He said what He said!" God will not change his mind about you or your gift regardless of what you do. Yes, you will experience more power if you submit to Him. Yes, it is dangerous to pursue purpose without the guidance of the One who gave it to you. He created you for the purpose, so He knows how it works best. Yes, the impact of your purpose will increase exponentially if you submit to the power of God's Spirit. He adds the super to your natural. You ain't seen power until you allow God's creative power to move freely in your brilliance! All that is true, but it is also true that nothing can stop your purpose from flowing. Not even you.

Gang leaders, psychic healers, and con men all use their brilliance. They were created with brilliance, and God will not take it back. In giving us free will, He leaves room for us to decide how we will use what He gave us, and He allows room for us to experience the consequences of our choices. He made you for your brilliance, and He will not take it away from you.

Your Brilliance Is a Perfect Fit

Your brilliance is a perfect fit for you. Although your brilliance will cost you something, it should not cost you everything. The innate, unique brilliance God prepared for you is specifically designed to fit you. You can do things that would overwhelm other people. You are capable of accomplishing goals that would never work for the next person. God specifically designed your personality and crafted your life to carry the specific brilliance He assigned to you.

In the New Living Translation of our foundational scripture, Jesus said,

> "Come to me, all of you who are weary and carry heavy burdens, and I will give you rest. Take my yoke upon you. Let me teach you, because I am humble and gentle at heart, and you will find rest for your souls. For my yoke is easy to bear, and the burden I give you is light" (Matthew 11:28-30).

Growing up in church, I heard this verse many times, but I never truly understood the power of it until I understood what a yoke is.

A yoke is a piece of farming equipment that connects two animals together for the purpose of tilling the soil. The yoke is used to train them as well as to connect them to their purpose. The yoke is fastened over the necks of the animals and then connected to the plow or cart they're assigned to pull. The yoke assists in carrying the weight of the plow or cart. To protect the animals, the yoke must be well-fitted. Plowing is not a punishment for the animals. They are too valuable to the farmer to be abused. Plowing is their purpose; it is what they were born to do. Therefore, the farmer carefully fits the appropriate yoke to each animal, adjusting as they grow, so they can do the work they were born to do without overextending or injuring themselves. In the same way, your brilliance is crafted specifically to fit you and to assist you in carrying the weight of your assignment.

In the same passage where Jesus referred to the yoke, He also talked about rest. We are created to rest and work. The only way for these two activities to successfully exist together is for you to submit to the yoke Jesus gives you, the brilliance assigned to you. Jesus said, "my yoke is easy to bear, and the burden I give you is light." (Matthew 11:30). Friend, I am convinced if the burden is heavy, it's not what God gave you. If you are overloaded and overwhelmed, you are carrying something God did not assign to your shoulders. The brilliance God assigned to you fits you perfectly and the load is light. That same load would crush someone else, but you are built for it. God values you too much to give you something that weighs too much for you to carry. You are too valuable to Him to be impaired. The brilliance God assigned to you is a perfect fit.

To bring quick relief to an overwhelmed society, burnout "experts" often offer Band-Aid level solutions to an area where deep trauma has occurred. *Disrupting Burnout* is not a shot-in-the-dark quick fix. It's a lifestyle shift that brings purpose and freedom. We disrupt burnout through the HeartWork strategies: three simple but powerful strategies that reveal and heal the root causes of burnout, launching you into a life of purpose and fulfillment. In the following chapters, you will become so acquainted with the HeartWork strategies that they'll be engrained into your being. Truth shared in these pages will free you from the habits that lead to overwhelm and burnout.

Do not read this book like a novel. Use it as a manual. Bookmark it, dogear pages, write notes in the margins, and highlight lines. This book will hold your stains and your tears. Use it so well that no one will ever want to borrow it. Download the *Disrupting Burnout* journal at patricebucknerjackson.com/journal to support your journey. Take the time to work through the exercises. Contemplate the questions and write out your answers. Note the thoughts that resonate with you on an index card and keep it in your purse. Ask questions. Think critically. Become a student of truth so you can be free.

In addition to journal prompts and questions within the chapters, at the end of each chapter, I'll invite you to "do the HeartWork." Each activity was created for you to apply the HeartWork strategies as you take this journey. I encourage you to slow down and complete each exercise. Pause to answer each journal question. This is not a book to be read; this is a manual to be practiced. The power of this journey is in the application of the strategies. Let's begin.

Do the HeartWork

When was the last time you felt like you truly made a positive impact on another person?

1. What did you do?
2. What was the impact on the other person or people?
3. What was the outcome of that experience?

Write about this experience in your down-loadable *Disrupting Burnout* journal found at patricebucknerjackson.com/journal.

Chapter 2

A Crisis of Brilliance

All my mentors told me I would be a vice president one day. Some even shared I could be university president if I desired. I never chased those titles, but it was always in my mind that they were possible for me. When I received a call from a mentor encouraging me to apply for a vice president position at a different university, I was honored but unsure. I'd recently been promoted and was very comfortable in my new position at my university. I felt like I grew up professionally at that institution and finally had the relationships, respect, and experience to move the needle on some things. It wasn't perfect, but I was comfortable. However, this call got my attention. Was it time to move? After twenty years, had I made it to the goal?

My husband, Edward, and I prayed. We discussed it with our parents and pastor. We even secretly drove to the new town to see how our spirits felt there. Our daughter was in her first semester of college in the town where we lived. Was it time to leave her? There were challenges at the new university. Was I ready for them?

After an interview process and much prayer and consideration, I accepted the job. We sold our home and moved to a new place. It felt like an adventure. It was the first time Edward and I had moved to a new city together, so we enjoyed having this adventure all to ourselves. In my new role, I had an experienced staff, passionate students, and an engaged community. I felt equipped for the task at hand.

Ten Months Later

I will never forget the day in August 2019 when I drove to work through the rain with my eyes filled with tears. I pulled into the reserved parking space with my title on it; that's what you get when you become vice president at a university. As a young professional, years earlier, I'd longed for one of those spots. That day, I sat in the car for a moment, attempting to compose myself. I wiped my eyes and freshened my make-up before walking into the building with my normal approach—singing good morning to students, greeting staff members, and giving hugs. It was all I could do to get behind the door of my corner office with the big picture windows. Finally alone, I crumbled. I held on to the edge of the wooden desk because I felt like I could no longer support my own weight. I really wanted to crawl under that desk and lie there in the fetal position. I fought that urge because I wouldn't have the strength to pull myself off the floor. Someone would find me there. What would they say? What would they think?

I felt trapped. I needed to leave, but I couldn't open that door. If I did, there would be a student who needed me, a staff member with a quick question, or a colleague who needed a moment of my time. Friend, the question is never quick, and the time is always longer than a moment. See, I had taught everyone in my life that I could be all things to all people, and they believed me. But I had nothing more to give.

When I was able to catch a moment of clarity, I picked up my phone and called Edward. After I explained what I was experiencing, my husband said, "Go home. I'll meet you there." I responded, "But I can't go home." Remember, Friend, it was August. If you're an educator, you know what August means. It's the busiest time of the year—moving students into residence halls, starting classes, resolving issues, consoling parents, rallying your team. August is *go* time! As I explained this conflict, Edward repeated his advice. "Go home. I will meet you there." I said "Okay."

I hung up the phone and wrote a letter to my president. I went to where she was in a meeting and waited outside the door until the meeting ended. When she opened the door, I handed her the letter and said, "Ma'am, I'm so sorry."

I quit.

At the beginning of the busiest season.

I quit.

With students and a large team who depended on me.

I quit.

Without proper notice or a plan.

I quit my job.

I am convinced to this day that I had no other choice. I felt in my heart if I came back one more day, someone would have to come get me instead of me walking out on my own power. I was done. I don't know what it feels like to lose your mind, but I am convinced I was close.

I went home. I didn't leave because I had another job lined up. I didn't leave because I had submitted my resume for other positions. I didn't leave temporarily, with a plan to return. I went home because I was broken and empty. I went home because I was burned out.

Five Months at Home

I was out of work for five months. It was the first time since I was twelve years old that I had no job and nothing to do. I sat at home looking at the dog and she looked back at me. It was the first time I'd stopped in my entire adult life. No work. No ministry. No mentoring. No speaking. My life came to a complete and abrupt halt. I experienced an involuntary, automatic shutdown. Everything stopped and I did not know what to do.

At first, I was angry. I was furious with everyone. *No one saw me struggling? Of all the people I helped, no one cared that I was hurting?* I spent weeks resenting my work and the way I'd worked. I was angry with God for bringing me to this place and with everyone else for applauding me along the way. I remained in this furious spiral until it hit me; this had happened before.

I had to acknowledge this was not the first time I'd experienced burnout. It was the worst, but not the first. I had experienced this feeling before but somehow found my way through it. In different seasons of my life, with different people and different jobs, I had burned out. So it wasn't them. It was me.

To add to my revelation, I realized my husband, my child, and very close friends had tried to reach out to me, but each time, I'd told them I was fine. I hid from them. In Edward's case, I argued him down that he just didn't understand what it meant to do my work. As for those who did not see me, it was because I did not allow them to see me. I wore overworking like a badge of honor. They didn't know my load was too heavy because I didn't allow them to know. I wore my professional mask gracefully even though it was killing me. I didn't allow people to help me because I am the helper. I made suffering look good, and the charade finally caught up with me.

What should I do now? Where will I work? Will higher education ever take me back? Should I work in a different industry? Do I have to start over? Did I just throw away twenty years of work?

I had so many questions and not enough answers. This was where prayer saved me. I reignited my spiritual life. I spent time in prayer and allowed myself to rest. The more I surrendered the clearer I became. To resolve my own burnout, I implemented the strategies I'll teach you here. And at the time of this writing, I have walked thousands of professional women through the same journey to purpose and freedom through my podcast, speaking, and coaching.

After five months, I went back to work. I was at a new university with a different title, associate vice president. In education, this is a step down from vice president, but it was necessary for me. I'd learned in those five months what my innate, unique brilliance is and where I fit best on a team. I intentionally sought a position that fit my purpose.

The work did not change. The pressure did not change. The demands had not changed. I changed. I approached work and life differently. I went back to work in January 2020, right in time to lead through the pandemic. It was the craziest time of my career, but I knew I was in the right place doing the right thing. I had new boundaries in place that allowed me to serve well without losing what means most to me. I served my students, built my team, and supported my leadership all while honoring and protecting me. It is possible, Friend. I'll show you how.

A Crisis of Brilliance

Before we begin this journey, I need to affirm your current position. Most accomplished women I meet at the beginning of this journey are in a season I call a Crisis of Brilliance. Allow me to give you language to describe and understand where you are. The most accurate comparison I can make is to a woman in the final stages of labor. You are exhausted. You

> *There is a shaking in your soul, and it is working for your good.*

feel pressure all around you. Pressure at home. Pressure at work. Pressure at church. It seems there is no space for relief. You may find yourself in a constant state of frustration. The work that once fulfilled you no longer feels like a good fit. You have a constant internal struggle with yourself, wondering if you will ever be at peace again. That personal struggle spills over to damage your closest relationships. This is the breaking and the shaking. It feels like no one and nothing you used to lean on for support is available to you any longer. You're disappointed because you've done all the things culture says you should do, and you still feel empty. You feel hoodwinked and bamboozled. You are accomplished and applauded in your community, but you feel like a complete failure in your heart. You feel like you're on a roller coaster, and you just want the ride to stop so you can get off.

Women stuck in a Crisis of Brilliance share sentiments like:

- "I feel like I'm losing my mind."
- "I pray, but I don't think He's listening."
- "I'm so angry, but I don't know why."
- "I just want to feel joy again."
- "I just feel like there's more." (This is the one I hear most often.)

Friend, you are not losing your mind. You have not done anything wrong. God is not punishing you. You are in a Crisis of Brilliance. Your entire story is being disrupted so normal falls away and brilliance comes forth. The brilliance God created on the inside of you is ready to shine forth. Brilliance is fighting its way through your trauma, grief, and limiting beliefs to get to the surface. Your brilliance is ready to be delivered, and your whole being is experiencing the pains of labor. You will make it. You will get to the other side of this. And on the other side, you will look back and see God's hand even in this. This book was especially written for you.

You need to know a few things about crisis. Crisis is not a creator, but it is a revealer and a magnifier. Another word for crisis is disruption. Just as the pandemic of 2020 revealed and magnified layers of chaos in America, a Crisis of Brilliance has a way of unearthing layers of experiences and beliefs you may not even know you're carrying. When Hurricane Katrina impacted the Gulf Coast, the flood caused caskets to arise from their buried place—a horrifying result. In the same way, your Crisis of Brilliance will cause things you have buried, like pain, soul wounds, and misaligned belief systems, to resurface. The shaking is necessary.

You cannot address what you cannot see. It's necessary for you to know what you carry. Your awareness of your own baggage is your first step toward freedom.

Friend, hear my heart. I know this season is uncomfortable. You don't feel like yourself. You want the crisis to end quickly. You wish things were back to normal, but I'm here to tell you this crisis is working in your favor. The Crisis of Brilliance did not come to destroy you. It came to reveal every thought, idea, memory, or belief holding you back as well as the hidden brilliance you have not yet encountered. There is a shaking in your soul, and it is working for your good.

God loves you too much to exalt you to a place your soul is not prepared to steward. He allows this shaking of the soul to come so everything attached to you that He did not send will fall away and what you will be left with is His reflection. Allow this spiritual surgery to occur so you can be healed. To show forth the glory of your Heavenly Father, you must be shaped into His image. This crisis did not come to break you. It came to make you.

You Are Not Too Late

God placed it in my heart to write a book several years ago. From that time until I started this book project, I felt shame and condemnation because I thought I was failing God. I made several attempts at writing this book but made no real progress. I thought God was tired of my disobedience in this area, and I was tired of myself. I wanted to give up on the idea completely, but it wouldn't leave my heart.

Now, I understand I couldn't have written this book any earlier. I share stories and experiences here that didn't happen until this year. I share revelation about our Heavenly Father that I didn't yet understand. God may have given you the vision a long time ago, but that doesn't mean it was the time to execute. Ecclesiastes 3:1 teaches us: "For everything there is a season, a time for every activity under heaven." Maybe you didn't finish your college degree. It was not your time. Maybe you delayed starting your business. It was not the season. Maybe God laid it on your heart to live in a different city, but you have not moved. Your time has not come.

When the time is right, you cannot deny it. You cannot stop the flow. I'm at a point now where this book wakes me up at night. I have a constant running list of updates on my phone as Holy Spirit speaks to me about this book every day. I've reached a point of no return. I couldn't stop this flow now if I tried. That's how you know it's time.

Friend, you are not too late. God knows how to get your attention. He knows how to push you in the right season and timing. Just like the taste of good soul food, the most impactful ideas take time to develop. When you hear God speak a new thing, follow up by asking Him, "How?" and "When?" If He says wait, put it in the crockpot of your soul, and watch Him develop the idea into His beautiful vision.

The Price of Going First

Your Crisis of Brilliance may be triggered by your role as the first. Maybe you are a first-generation college graduate or a first-time entrepreneur in your family. Maybe you are the first to hold a marriage together or the first to come to Christ. You may be the first woman in a certain organization or the first person of color. Yes, even in the twenty-first century, there are still so many firsts.

I realized I was first as I sat with the interviewer for a local magazine. One of their questions, for which I was unprepared, shocked me. "How does it feel to be the first female dean of students in the history of Georgia Southern University?" The only answer I had at that moment was: "I didn't realize I was the first." After over one hundred years of history at my beloved university, I was the first woman to hold my position. I never set out to make history. It was not my goal to shatter any glass ceiling. I just took one step of obedience at a time and found myself first.

I want to honor the price paid by the pioneer. There is extreme pressure in going first. As a young professional, I asked one of my mentors, "Why is it so hard?" in reference to my professional path. She looked me in the eyes and said, "It's never easy when you're clearing a path for others to follow. You must cut the road through the wilderness so others can follow safely. Going first will always cost you more."

Pioneers in a new land make all the mistakes, learn the hard lessons, battle unknown threats, and invest hard work to prepare the land for those coming after them. If you are a first, I want to acknowledge the weight on your shoulders. I honor the price you pay to pave the way for folks coming after you. And I want you to know you can rest here. You can catch your breath. You don't need to perform or accomplish anything. This is the place where you can find relief in the journey. This is the place where you can heal from the toil. I see you. You're safe here.

A Call to Transition

Regardless of how you arrived at this point of crisis, I want you to know you do not have to escape. You don't have to run. When I left my job without notice, I fled. I was so broken that I had no other choice. But guess what, Friend. My escape did not resolve my crisis. I just took the crisis with me from the corner office to my home. I still had to walk through these HeartWork strategies to get through the crisis.

I cannot tell you how many women I've encountered who are convinced that if they just get a new job all will be well. Friend, you may leave a place, but you take you with you. The crisis is in you. The shaking is in your soul. A work environment may amplify your crisis, but it is never the source. The job may or may not be the right place for you, but you don't even know that until you disrupt the Cycle of Burnout.

We need to do some work together before you start making life-altering decisions. If you are in an abusive or otherwise unhealthy situation, seek the support of an HR professional, counselor, pastor, or trusted friend immediately. Otherwise, let's walk through the strategies together until your next step is so clear you cannot avoid it. You don't have to escape. You can transition safely from burnout to brilliance by allowing your soul to heal.

Will You Pray with Me?

Father, I come to You on behalf of my sister who is spiraling in a Crisis of Brilliance. Make your presence known to her at this moment. Remind her that you are with her and have never left.

Allow her to physically feel the tangible presence of your Spirit with her in this moment. Change her perspective and allow her to see this season of life from your eyes. Help her see how this shaking is working for her and not against her. Allow the shaking to release the hold of every idea, thought, memory, and belief system that has held her captive. Replace those misaligned thoughts with your thoughts about her. Convince her in a miraculous way that she is not alone. Hold her close at this moment and walk her into true freedom. I know you will because you did it for me. All these petitions I ask and declare in the matchless name of Jesus Christ.

Amen.

Do the Heart Work

Download the *Disrupting Burnout* journal for a fillable copy of this activity at patricebuckner jackson.com/journal

Visualize this.

Imagine you are standing in the center of a dark box. You can see light through the cracks in the box, but you're trapped inside. Really look around at the box that has tried to hold you hostage. Think about the unfruitful lessons you've learned, the negative words you've heard, and the stories you've created in your own mind.

You need to take down that box! Good thing you have some tools in there with you. Notice the ladder in the corner, the sledgehammer in your hand, the helmet on your head, and the protective goggles on your eyes. You had more resources than you were aware of. Let's get to work!

Grab the sledgehammer, climb the ladder, and take down that ceiling of perfectionism. Hit it hard and watch it fall! No need to be neat about it. You won't need that where you're going.

Now, come down the ladder, noticing the debris all around your feet.

Next, take down the dark wall of shame. Think about all the labels you've carried throughout your life that caused you to hide. Notice the light bursting through as you destroy shame.

Now go after the wall of "not enough." Destroy every experience that makes you feel like you are not enough. Take down that dark wall! Notice the walls of overwhelm and overworking falling on their own. You took out the supporting walls, so everything else just falls at your feet.

Finally, walk away from the box and see the brilliant future ahead of you. Are you ready to live in freedom for real?

After completing this Demo Day visualization exercise, answer the following prompts in your *Disrupting Burnout* journal:

1. What other walls have held you captive?
2. Where did those walls come from? What experiences led to you constructing those walls in your life?
3. What light do you see as you emerge from the box? What life are you walking into?

Chapter 3

Disrupting Burnout

When interviewing potential clients, I always ask, "What will happen if you don't do anything to break this cycle?" I have heard a variety of responses. Some women share how they've gained weight or lost their appetite. Others share how they battle addictions or have lost significant relationships. Several women have voiced that they feel like they are holding on by a thread. The comment that concerns me most is "This will cost me my life." The statement itself is alarming, but the frequency that I hear this statement compels me to do something about it. Professional women are suffering physically, mentally, emotionally, and relationally to the point that their lives are in danger. They are battling high blood pressure, depression, anxiety, low self-esteem, imposter syndrome, isolation and a host of other challenges as a result of burnout. The Cycle of Burnout is detrimental, and we must disrupt the cycle.

> *"This will cost me my life."*

I refer to recovery from burnout as "disrupting burnout," which is also the name of my podcast. I use the term disrupt because its meaning most clearly defines our goal here. A quick Google search for "definition of disrupt" produced the following definition from Oxford Languages, "drastically alter or destroy the structure of."[1] In offering the origin of the word, Oxford Languages provides the Latin root word "disrumpere" which means "broken apart."[1] The Cambridge Dictionary states disrupt means to "prevent something, especially a system, process, or event, from continuing as usual or as expected."[2] My goal for you is not that you just step out of burnout. If you merely step out, you may just as easily step back in. My goal is for you to radically change and drastically alter your negative core belief systems. On this journey, you will destroy the Cycle of Burnout in your life so you can live in brilliance.

Cycle of Burnout

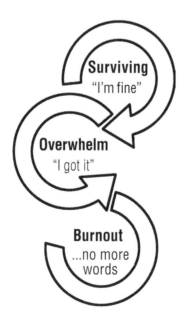

Surviving

I discuss burnout in terms of cycles because that is exactly what happens for those of us who are prone to burnout. In one moment, you feel fine. You are surviving. In surviving mode, the first part of the cycle, you're holding it all together. Your calendar is full, but you're handling things. You're doing too much and feeling the pressure, but you're maintaining. Your focus is on everyone else in your life. You have many obligations, and you're not quite sure how to stop. You could really use a rest, but you fear the whole house of cards may fall if you step away. In the surviving phase, everything is "fine." Life is just "fine." You know something is missing, but you can't put your finger on it.

How's work? "Fine."

How are you feeling today? "I'm fine."

Hey, Friend, is everything okay? "Yep, everything is fine."

"Fine" is always a sign when I'm coaching women. When everything is "fine," I know the cycle has begun. You were not created to be "fine." According to John 10:10, Jesus came so you may experience life in abundance until it overflows. "Fine" does not meet that standard.

Overwhelm

If you don't make a change while in surviving mode, you will easily find yourself in the next phase of the Cycle of Burnout, overwhelm. In overwhelm, you feel the water level of your life rising as you struggle to keep your head above the waves. Overwhelm is the prelude to burnout, during which you really need help, but you're afraid to ask for it. You battle thoughts of insignificance and incompetence.

You begin to feel not good enough, not strong enough, not smart enough—not enough.

People in tune with you may notice you struggling. They may even check on you, but you push their concern away for fear of being exposed. In overwhelm, you begin to manifest negative consequences of living an overwhelmed life. Your body, soul, and Spirit send you warning signs in overwhelm. (Please note: I capitalize Spirit because this is the God part of you.) Everything in you is trying to get your attention. Red lights are flashing, and the warning sirens are blaring. A shutdown is pending. You may begin to retreat into isolation just to catch your breath. In overwhelm, you try to convince yourself you can handle it. "I got it!" becomes your mantra.

Can I help you? "I got it."

Need to take something off your plate? "I got it."

Are you okay? "I'm good. I got it."

"I got it" is a stiff arm extended to keep people away. In overwhelm, you reject the support you desperately need. You're afraid to allow anyone to get too close. You're concerned about what they might think if they truly saw the mess behind the mask. You try to protect the trust and respect others have for you by keeping them at a distance. The mess piles up around you, but you wouldn't dare allow anyone to see it.

The mess may be metaphorical or physical. Stacks of paperwork piled up under my desk, at one point in my career, so many that I could no longer put my legs under that desk. Any quick movement, and the avalanche of my overwhelm would fall all over the floor. So many people came into that beautiful

Overwhelm is the whisper, but burnout is the demand!

office with the huge windows and never saw the mess. I didn't feel safe letting them see that side of me. I was overwhelmed and afraid.

Burnout

You will stop when burnout hits. Burnout is forced shutdown. It is involuntary. Burnout is automatic. Burnout is inconvenient. You cannot plan for the shutdown. It just happens. Overwhelm is the whisper, but burnout is the demand. In this phase, you can no longer hold it together. Something breaks, and the damage cannot be hidden. Your body, soul, and Spirit are all exhausted. Your most significant relationships are strained, and clutter fills your environment. Even if you want to keep pushing, you can't. You just do not have it in you anymore.

Burnout manifests in different ways for different people. My friend Lindsay Rae Perry of Journey to CEO describes how she collapsed in the street, not knowing who she was or where she lived. Another good friend, who serves as a transformational capacity coach, Nicole Rhone, describes how she ended up in the hospital after shouldering a demanding corporate job and a work commute that took several hours each day. I walked away from my twenty-year career with no income and no plan. Some people turn to substance abuse or fall into depression. Burnout stops you in your tracks. You are forced to stop, and there are no more words. There's nothing more to say at this point because you're too tired to even speak. This is rock bottom.

In the Gallup Workforce Panel survey of February 2022,[3] 76% of employees report they experience burnout at least sometimes. K-12 education professionals report the highest level of burnout of all professions at 44%. When we extract teachers from that group, the number increases to 51% reporting they "very often" or "always" feel burned out at work. College and university professionals rank second most burned out at 35%. Thirty-four percent of all professionals who identify as female across all professions report they "very often" or "always" feel burned out at work compared to 26% of professionals who identify as male. Most research on burnout is focused on caring professions like teaching, nursing, and social work. The body of research concerning burnout in the medical profession is growing day by day.[4] In addition, there is new research on burnout among parents[5] and caregivers.[6] Contemporary research shows there is a burnout epidemic, but the traditional definitions of burnout are sorely lacking.

Disrupting Burnout Is Not

In 2019, the World Health Organization (WHO) included burnout in the eleventh revision of the International Classification of Diseases (ICD-11) as an "occupational phenomenon" and called it "a syndrome conceptualized as resulting from chronic workplace stress that has not been successfully managed." According to the WHO, burnout "refers specifically to phenomena in the occupational context and should not be applied to describe experiences in other areas of life."[7]

The WHO definition was derived from the work of Christina Maslach, Michael Leiter, and Susan Jackson who developed the Maslach Burnout Inventory in 1981. These researchers define burnout as a "psychological syndrome emerging as a prolonged response to chronic interpersonal stressors on the job." They found "the three key dimensions of this response are overwhelming exhaustion, feelings of cynicism and detachment from the job, and a sense of ineffectiveness and lack of accomplishment."[8]

Although I respect this research, my experience has taught me burnout should not be limited to the work context. I have not met one client who only experiences burnout and overwhelm at work. I've had more than one client who says work provides them with respite from the overwhelming parts of their life. My clients experience the key dimensions mentioned above in parenting, in marriage, in caregiving, in their family roles, in serving at church, and the list goes on. I have clients who have left an overwhelming work environment to pursue working for themselves and still struggle with burnout.

Work is often not the original onset of the Cycle of Burnout for my clients. Many of them can trace overwhelm back to middle school or high school. You can burn out in ministry even if ministry is not your primary occupation. You can burn out on a passion. You can burnout while serving your purpose. Burnout is invasive; it impacts every part of your life. Burnout is a thief; it comes to steal and destroy everything that means the most to you. Burnout is deeper than workplace factors. Burnout is a heart issue. Its root system is stored in your belief system. Surface tactics bring temporary relief but leave you vulnerable to recurrence. Recovery from burn-

You do not have to wait for the workplace to change for you to be well.

out is deeper than workplace culture, time management, resilience, and work-life balance. In my study of burnout recovery, these are the typical areas of focus, and each one falls short of a remedy in one way or another. To disrupt the Cycle of Burnout for good, you must do the HeartWork. Let's look more closely at why standard strategies so often fail to resolve burnout.

Workplace Culture

Changing your workplace culture is not the solution for your burnout. Workplace culture can be a major contributor to burnout, but it's not the solution. Even if your work culture changed for the good today, the damage is done, and your body keeps a record. Your workplace may create an environment for burnout to flourish, and it's probable your job is a major contributor to your burnout. Your workplace may also add to your personal trauma, magnifying the risk and extent of your burnout. However, you do not have to wait for a culture shift in your industry before disrupting your burnout.

I've had clients who still struggled with burnout and overwhelm after leaving a toxic work environment. When we traced their steps, we found a history of survival and overwhelm even prior to the toxic job. And after their transition out of the toxic space, they still needed the HeartWork strategies to locate and address the root of the problem in their hearts. Some people are drawn to toxic work environments because of the firestorm they carry in their soul. If you go from job to job and you always find yourself surrounded by chaos, you need to ask yourself why you continue to be attracted to those environments. If you've worked in a toxic work environment for a long time, why do you stay? You may need to leave that place, but do not expect another workplace to heal you.

Even when you leave, you take you with you. That baggage goes where you go. Your workplace may be the catalyst of your crisis, and institutions, schools, and organizations have a responsibility to promote and support wellness for their employees in measurable ways. However, you do not have to wait for the workplace to change for you to be well. If they start prioritizing wellness today, you still need the HeartWork strategies to recover from the impact of your journey so far. If they never prioritize wellness, the HeartWork strategies will be your healing, your protection, and your guide as you continue to navigate challenging environments.

You are your first advocate. Take the responsibility of protecting your peace back into your own hands. Do not hand your right to be well over to an industry. Decide to be free now, whether the culture changes or not. The HeartWork strategies will teach you how.

Calendar Tactics

Disrupting burnout is not about calendar tactics. Many great books out there focus on managing your calendar, but this is not one of them. I wrote an e-book on the topic several years ago, but I have to let you know none of those tactics prevented burnout. Burnout is more about the quality of engagements on your calendar than the quantity of engagements. I have more responsibilities today than I did when I was overwhelmed and burned out. The difference is everything I do today flows from my unique brilliance and is secured by my boundaries. Therefore, I do not overwork, and I do not work outside of my innate, unique value. Anytime I attempt to step out of those boundaries, I immediately feel misaligned, and I run back to safety. So this is not the place where you will learn to manage your calendar. This journey is deeper work.

Resilience

More resilience is not the solution for burnout either. Most of the proclaimed experts I hear speak on burnout immediately resort to a session on resilience. In my work coaching professional women, I've found you do not need another lesson in resilience. You know how to fall and get back up. You know how to be pushed into a corner and fight your way out. You know how to pull yourself up by your bootstraps. You know how to keep pushing in the face of adversity. Your problem is not lack of resilience. The problem is you've had to be resilient too often. You have bounced back so much your bounce-back is broken.

You know how to fight. You know how to bounce back. You know how to be resilient. I didn't write this book to teach you how to be resilient. The woman this book is written for does not need another lesson in resilience. You're already good at that. Maybe too good.

New Normal

Disrupting burnout is not about rushing into a "new normal." Human beings don't like to remain in discomfort. We prefer to fix it or mask it and move on. A premature new normal that ignores the need to recover is not the solution for burnout. Through my doctoral research, I studied the five phases of crisis management according to FEMA.[9] The fifth phase of this process is recovery, during which you heal and rebuild. Human beings often want to skip this step.

After 2020, many people wanted to rush to a new normal where we didn't have to wear masks or walk around in fear for our health. After a divorce, a woman desires to create a new normal for herself and her children that masks the impact of the split. After the loss of a child, a mother desires the grieving process to end so she can live without the constant pain in her heart. After the abuse ends, a survivor desires to move on with her life like it never happened. You may desire to skip the pain of recovery in your story.

Imagine there was a hurricane in your area yesterday. Today the rain has stopped, and the winds have ceased. Would you look at your neighbor and say, "Go back into your flooded house and be normal"? I imagine you think that sounds ridiculous. The same applies to prematurely rushing into a new normal after trauma. So much has changed. You need to recover. So no, Friend, rushing into some version of normal after your burnout crisis will not disrupt your burnout.

Work-Life Balance

Finally, Friend, we will not focus on work-life balance. During my "Disrupting Burnout" workshops, it never fails that someone, normally several folks, mention their need for balance. Let me show you why work-life balance is not the answer. Imagine every responsibility in your life is a dumbbell. Now imagine holding all your weight at the same time for an extended period. Holding them in your mind. Holding them in your heart. Trying to hold all the things, all the time, all at once. Eventually, something will fall. And when weighty things fall, damage occurs. You may get hurt. Someone you love could get hurt.

How often have you asked someone, "How are you?" and they answered, "I'm just tired"? "I'm just tired" doesn't necessarily mean that person needs a nap. "I'm just tired" means: "I'm worn out from carrying all my stuff, at the same time, all the time." Balance is not realistic, not sustainable, and not a fair expectation. It's a myth of strength. No person, not even the strongest woman, can carry everything all at the same time and still be okay. So balancing work and life is not the solution to burnout.

Disrupting Burnout Strategies

There are three proven strategies that truly disrupt the Cycle of Burnout for good:

1. Check your baggage.
2. Build your boundaries.
3. Discover your brilliance.

Notice these are strategies, not sequential steps. You might work on all three strategies at the same time or dig deeply into one strategy while the other two run in the background. These strategies are not a "one and done" solution; they are a lifestyle. As you evolve in purpose, you'll revisit the strategies as a form of quality control in your life. Disrupting burnout requires constantly walking through these three strategies.

Each strategy is rooted in scripture. This journey is an intimate walk through your soul with Holy Spirit. If you experience distress or triggering emotions during this journey, stop, and take note of the feelings. What triggered the feelings? What sensations do they create? Where do you feel them in your body? Take those notes to a therapist or other licensed professional who can help you process what's coming up for you. Allow the Word of God to restore the life He created you to live.

Our foundational scripture comes from Matthew 11:28-30, which is stated so beautifully in The Message translation:

> Are you *tired*? *Worn out*? *Burned out* on religion? Come to me. Get away with me and you'll *recover your life*. I'll show you how to take a *real rest*. Walk with me and work with me—watch how I do it. Learn the *unforced rhythms of grace*. I won't lay anything *heavy or ill-fitting* on you. Keep company with me and you'll *learn to live freely and lightly*. (Emphasis added.)

We will study this scripture along with several others throughout this journey.

Friend, regardless of where you are today, you can recover from burnout. You can disrupt the Cycle of Burnout so you never have to hit rock bottom again. You can discover the life you were created to live. You can live in purpose and freedom by checking your baggage, building your boundaries, and discovering your brilliance. Let's work through each strategy together.

Do the Heart Work

How are you? No, really. I want to know. More importantly, I want you to know. How often we ask this question in passing, just as a greeting, but not really wanting an answer. One of the greatest mistakes I made was never checking in with myself. I was so consumed with the needs of others that I completely ignored my own needs. Friend, before we begin this journey, I need you to check in with you. You need an answer today.

I want to challenge you to do a little self-assessment, a bit of a walkthrough to answer the question "How are you?" right now. If you're willing and if you're safe to do so, sit comfortably with both feet on the floor. Close your eyes for a moment and take a deep cleansing breath. Take another breath. Open your eyes. Now take just a few minutes to answer the following questions in your journal or workbook. Do not edit your thoughts. This is just for you, so no need to judge yourself. Write exactly what comes to your heart.

Here we go.

How's your body? How are you feeling physically? Are you accommodating any ache or pain? Does any system or function in your body seem just a bit off? Have you been ignoring any medical concerns? How's your body?

How's your mind? What thoughts do you think as you wake in the morning? What thoughts do you think as you attempt to rest at night? What thoughts do you push away as you work during the day because you don't have time to deal with them? How's your mind?

How's your heart? Not the heart that beats, but the heart that feels. What emotions are you wrestling with? Have you had reactions that feel outside of your personality? Is there any unresolved anger, shame, fear, or confusion in your life? Do you find your emotional reactions are out of control? How's your heart?

How are your relationships? I'm talking about the ones that mean the most to you. Think about the relationships you want to be with you forever. Is there any discord or division? Are you experiencing any break in communication with the ones you love? Is there any relationship you feel like you're losing? How are your relationships?

 Download the *Disrupting Burnout* journal for a fillable copy of this activity at patricebuckner jackson.com/journal or scan the QR code for access.

Chapter 4

Living in Alignment

I've learned so much about alignment through visits with chiropractors over the years. For instance, I now know chiropractors focus on the spine because all the nerves in your body are connected there. The brain and spinal cord act as the central operating system for the body, taking in information, processing that information, and sending back instructions for response through the nervous system. Every system, organ, and cell in your body is somehow connected to the spinal cord, which communicates with the brain.

I was amazed how an adjustment to my spine alleviated pain in my wrist, and how numbness of my hand had nothing to do with my hand, but the source was a compressed nerve in my back. I discussed infertility with my chiropractor and learned how certain adjustments had positive impacts on my reproductive system. I also experienced how an appropriate adjustment to my spine would clear up congestion in my respiratory system. A chiropractor noticed a misalignment in my spine and then touched a tender spot elsewhere in my body that I didn't even know was injured.

A misaligned spine can block the communication between the brain and the body, causing numbness, pain, or paralysis. My chiropractor taught me just as we take our car in to have the tires aligned after so many miles, our bodies need similar attention due to daily wear and tear. As an adjustment with a chiropractor impacts the wellness of your entire body, an adjustment in your belief system impacts the wellness of your soul.

It felt miraculous when my lower back pain resolved itself as I walked through the HeartWork strategies. Some days I couldn't even walk my dog due to the pain, but I haven't experienced that since implementing these strategies. I was carrying more in my heart than I was on my back. My invisible backpack was overflowing, and I felt it physically.

Have you checked your invisible backpack today? All of us have one. We put it on every day. Your invisible backpack is full of all your experiences. Everything you've learned, formally and informally, all major life events, and all your beliefs, ideas, systems, and constructs are in that invisible backpack. If you're honest, you may have more than a backpack. Some of us drag large roller bags or emotional trunks around every day. Your baggage determines how you engage with the world. The weight of your invisible luggage blocks your access to brilliance and causes soul injuries you cannot see.

The backpack itself is not good or bad. It's just the container. Each of us is responsible for opening that container, becoming acquainted with the contents, and doing some spring cleaning every now and then to lighten the load. Remove what no longer fits and replace it with beliefs that align with who you truly are.

This is the first HeartWork strategy we need to discuss: check your baggage.

Check Your Baggage

The goals of checking your baggage are to: 1) remove thoughts, ideas, beliefs, and systems that promote burnout and 2) replace those misaligned beliefs with thought systems that promote brilliance. In checking your baggage, you make adjustments in your soul to release your brilliance. If your belief systems are faulty, your brilliance is in jeopardy of overexposure, overperformance, and damage. If your belief systems are misaligned, it causes a disconnection between your brilliance and your actions. Brilliance is always there, but a blockage hinders the flow.

Misalignment in your soul also leads to a disconnect between the soul and your Spirit. Think of it this way, there are three parts to every human being: the body, the soul, and the Spirit. According to Genesis 2:7, God ". . . formed man of the dust of the ground [body] and breathed into his nostrils the breath of life [Spirit]; and man became a living [soul]." The word soul there, in the original Hebrew, means mind, will, imagination, and emotions.[1] Therefore, misalignment in your soul means disorder in your mind, will, imagination, and emotions. Chaos in your mind, will, imagination and emotions causes you to disconnect from Spirit, and your body behaves accordingly. Therefore, to have peace in your mind, stay connected to your Spirit, and take action in your brilliance, you must make adjustments in your soul. In checking your baggage, you will determine where your soul needs an adjustment.

Checking your baggage is about adjusting your belief system. This doesn't mean you need to toss every belief away and start over. Those beliefs that serve you well and align with God's thoughts about you should not change; these ideas hold you steady, especially in troubled times. As you check your baggage, you become aware of what you carry and make intentional decisions about what you will continue to carry. Weights like shame, guilt, unforgiveness, low self-esteem, insecurity, and malice are too heavy, and they hinder you from becoming the woman God created you to be. Those beliefs weigh your backpack down and hinder your progress. So many women believe they're not enough because they have not seen the progress they desire in their lives. Friend, you are more than enough! Your current load is just too heavy for progress.

It's time to lay something aside. After identifying weight that must be removed from your baggage, you need to replace misaligned thoughts with beliefs in harmony with who God created you to be. Throughout this process, you have no one to impress. In fact, as you work in this area, you'll become less impressed with titles, degrees, accolades, and expectations. Freedom is the primary goal. I'm talking about the kind of freedom you find in God. Remove every layer until there's nothing left but how He made you. Imperfectly perfect. Whole. Healed. Free.

In this process, you remove misaligned thoughts and replace them with belief systems that align with God's Word for you. Don't stop with removing; negative thoughts must be replaced. The entire process is necessary. Too many women become aware of misaligned beliefs and stop at removing those beliefs, leaving critical areas of their backpack empty. This leaves room for destructive belief systems to return with a vengeance.

In Matthew 12:43-45, Jesus taught:

> "When an evil spirit leaves a person, it goes into the desert, seeking rest but finding none. Then it says, 'I will return to the person I came from.' So it returns and finds its former home empty, swept, and in order. Then the spirit finds seven other spirits more evil than itself, and they all enter the person and live there. And so that person is worse off than before."

In the same way, you must replace misaligned thoughts with a mindset that fits your purpose. In this journey to brilliance, you will learn how to rid yourself of misaligned thoughts and how to accept and act upon purposeful thoughts.

Checking your backpack is about building upon a solid foundation. I love to watch renovation shows on HGTV where professionals transform a space that's run down and sometimes unlivable into an oasis in a matter of weeks. One thing I've noticed about renovations is they always start with the foundation. If the contractors notice any defect in the foundation, those issues must be repaired before any other construction can commence. These folks understand building upon a faulty foundation is a waste of time, effort, and money. It does not matter how beautiful the space is in the end if the foundation is cracked, weak, or faulty. In checking your backpack, you deconstruct every misaligned system, belief, or behavior and replace it with thoughts that align with your purpose so you can build brilliance on a strong foundation.

Checking your backpack is also about healing. As you face the contents of your backpack, you may experience a variety of emotions. It's fascinating how we adapt to accommodate a heavy load. Don't be surprised if checking your backpack reveals soul injuries you were not aware of. Just like your body may adapt to work around a physical injury, your mind and heart adapt to carry soul injuries. It's possible you have adapted for so long that you're no longer aware of the original injury. I must warn you, Friend, adapting to cover an injury always causes damage in other areas. Therefore, it's imperative you dig deeply into your backpack to reveal and heal all wounds.

Healing Is a Messy Process

Edward and I learned a lot about healing over the last three years. In 2020, Edward discovered a painful abscess on the back of his neck. The cyst grew to the point that he couldn't sleep well or turn his neck without excruciating pain. This was a tiny growth compared to the mass of his entire body, but this tiny growth impacted everything for him. It was difficult to think about anything else because the pain was so invasive.

After consulting with his primary care physician and a specialist, we decided to have the abscess removed. The specialist presented it as an easy in-office procedure with about one week of recovery. This decision seemed like a no-brainer, considering the level of discomfort my husband was experiencing. Edward also decided to undergo the procedure without anesthesia as he historically had a hard time waking up after surgery. The doctor reluctantly agreed, but warned Edward the procedure would be extremely uncomfortable with just a localized pain reducer. We all agreed on a plan, and we set a date.

The procedure only took about half an hour and the doctor reported it was a success. He gave me some instructions for at-home care and sent us on our way. That's where the healing lessons began. My first obstacle in this healing process was to look at the wound. Before I could serve my husband and care for the wound, I had to fight through my personal aversion to looking at it. Now let me give a shout out to all the nurses, all the medical attendants, all the nurse assistants, the PAs, the doctors, hospital custodians, and everyone else who works in healthcare. Thank you from the bottom of my heart because—let me tell you something—healthcare is not my ministry. However, I was willing to do it because I love that man. I had to look at it before I could take care of it. I had to know what it should look like and recognize signs of danger.

One morning several days after the procedure, I felt like something was wrong with the wound. I couldn't name the problem, but I could tell by looking at it that something was off. So many thoughts raced through my mind. *Maybe I'm being extra. Maybe I'm being anxious. Maybe it's no big deal.* I tried to push those thoughts away, but I couldn't rest. At the point of tears, I told my husband, "We've got to go to your doctor because something isn't right."

What a day! We couldn't get in to see the primary care physician or the specialist who had done the procedure. We finally ended up in a local wound care center, and I am so glad God led us there. The medical team reassured us we'd done the right thing by coming to them. There was a problem with the wound, but they were able to mitigate infection and get us back on track with healing.

I'm so glad I trusted my gut that day. You must be brave enough to look at the wound and trust your gut when something isn't right. It's time to acknowledge where you've been wounded. Look at the hurt. Look at the pain. Look at the offense. Before you can do anything about it, you must be able to look at the ugliness. Holy Spirit led you here because, in your heart, you know something is not right. From the outside you look like the picture of success, but inside you're carrying wounds that need attention. No more covering. No more pretending. See your pain for what it is.

Edward and I needed help in this process. The wound was in a spot he couldn't see for himself, so he needed somebody there who was willing to help him. In the doctor's office right after the initial procedure, the doctor brought me in and said, "Okay, let me show you what you need to do to care for the wound." He took me step by step through the process, teaching me how to take care of this wound for my husband. This was a new experience and I needed coaching to do it well. I learned from the doctor that day, and I did some research on my own to strengthen my approach and make sure I was helping Edward and not hurting him.

When you're going through a healing process, especially one you're not familiar with, you need support. Choosing to take a healing journey alone significantly decreases your odds of success. At the least, you waste time learning hard lessons that a guide could have helped you avoid. At the worst, you end up with more extensive damage due to ignorance. This is why I wrote this book—to give you some of those lessons. This is also why coaching is essential. A coach has knowledge, skills, ability, and experience to guide you through the process of disrupting burnout, helping you avoid pitfalls and supporting you as you pursue freedom. Do not take this journey alone. You have help available to you.

Healing will cost you. Edward and I had to invest in healing supplies. I had no idea of all the wound-care products on the market prior to this experience. Without even realizing it, we created our own little formulary. We bought bandages and wraps and gloves and ointment and fancy scissors I'd never used before. We had it all because, to take care of the wound, I needed the appropriate resources ready and available. In addition to the supplies, we had medical bills from the procedure and the follow-ups, and we invested more than money in those appointments. We both had to wake up earlier each morning to have time to attend to the wound before leaving for work. We also made time each night for wound care.

You cannot just talk about healing, Friend. You must have some skin in the game. What are you willing to give? What is your investment? Are you willing to read this entire book? Are you willing to stop and answer the journal prompts? Will you reserve time in your schedule to walk through this process? Will you invest in a coaching group or one-on-one coaching to get the support you need in this process? Are you willing to be honest with yourself? Can you see how holding on to the pain is costing you more than healing ever will? What are you willing to give to support your own healing process?

In Edward's healing process, I had to change my definition of beautiful. Friend, remember medicine is not my ministry, and this thing was rough. In the early days, I had to pump myself up just to remove the bandage: "You can do this, Patrice! It's not as bad as yesterday. It's getting better every day." As we walked through the healing process, however, the wound became beautiful to me. It was never a pretty sight. I never added it to my Instagram feed, but watching things get better became my new definition of beautiful.

As time went by, I became less squeamish about looking at the wound. I began to see the beauty in the process. I noticed details that gave me clues that we were headed in the right direction. I watched the miraculous power of the human body to heal itself.

I was a witness as new skin cells formed and replaced damaged skin. I observed as the pain subsided and Edward began to return to himself. I had a front row seat to the miraculous power of God that no one else had.

One day, a family member saw the wound for the first time. A few months had passed since the procedure, and there was no more bandage. Although much healing had occurred by that point, that family member physically shuddered at the sight of the healed area. Their reaction surprised me because all I could think about was how far we had come.

Be careful who you allow to see your wounds. Other people may look at your progress and fail to appreciate it. They weren't there in the hardest times. They didn't see the tears you cried, the layers you shed, or the process you've been through. We prayed over that wound. We shed some tears in that process. We saw God answer our prayers for healing. We are no longer impressed by aesthetics. The healing process is hard. It is messy, and it is beautiful.

The healing process is also irritating. There's itching, irritation, and some smelly stuff that happens when your body is healing. Edward really wanted to scratch his wound to relieve the itch, but scratching would have made it more irritated. At a certain point, it was getting on his nerves. He was tired of carrying it, and honestly, I was tired of caring for it. Although we were both ready to be done, I realized the irritation was a sign that the healing process was coming to an end. The itching and irritation increased as the healing progressed. The more the wound healed, the more it irritated my husband.

Like giving birth, the most painful part is right before your breakthrough. Do not get weary in your healing. Stay connected to someone who will coach you and support you in the moments you want to give up. Remember the irritation is a sign that healing is almost complete. You've come a long way, Friend. Don't give up now.

I need you to know healing often takes longer than you want it to take. The doctor initially told us we would deal with this wound for seven days. Seven days went by, and the wound wasn't healed. One week after that, we were still doing wound care. The healing process took much longer than we planned. We were still in it when it was no longer a hot topic for family and friends. So many people reached out to us when Edward first had the procedure. However, those folks eventually moved on to think about other things, as they should, and we were still healing. We continued caring for the wound until it seemed like the healing was complete.

We rejoiced the first day Edward went with no bandage. However, the celebration was short-lived because we learned the first procedure hadn't gone deep enough, so we had to do it again. Edward had to be sedated, and it took months for him to heal from the second surgery. After we got through the second healing—months of wound care, and finally, everything was sealed up, no more bandages—we learned he had to go into surgery for a third time. This time he had two procedures, two weeks apart.

If you're counting, that's four surgeries in two years. It was exhausting. It stretched us to our limits. It felt like it would never end. However, I am happy to say we finally have a solution, a prescribed medication that resolved the problem. All the surgeries could have been avoided if we'd known about this from the beginning. That part would frustrate me if I didn't believe the surgeries were necessary steppingstones to get us to the solution. We would never have considered this medication if we hadn't experienced such a journey with the surgeries. Friend, everything you've gone through to this point got you here. Do not despise your challenges. They gave you the push you needed to run into HeartWork.

Maybe you've tried program after program or coach after coach and you haven't found what you need. Looking at the time elapsed and the money spent could cause you to feel frustrated except the truth is all those steps led you here. That frustration pushed you to the point that you are open and willing to take this journey. You learned so much through your healing. You built muscles you didn't know you needed. Now you are ready for resolution. You are ready to release hurt, pain, shame, and anger to fully embrace the woman you were created to be. Do not despise the pain that brought you this far. Maybe it's not a physical wound for you. Maybe your wound is deeper. Soul injuries tend to hide longer and therefore take more time to heal. Every step of your journey so far was purposed to get you here. Appreciate the journey. Honor your path by stepping into true healing. It's a messy process, but it's necessary, Friend.

Checking your backpack may be especially difficult if you carry traumatic experiences. Deep trauma may include abuse of any kind, traumatic loss, critical illness, or any life-altering circumstance. To reveal and heal deep trauma from your past, I recommend counseling. You need someone trained and licensed to help you navigate deep wounds.

Through counseling, I was able to understand the roots of my trauma, and I learned how to clear those roots from my backpack so I am no longer driven by them. There's great freedom in understanding your source of struggle and taking control of that area of your life. I walked students to counseling for over twenty years before I went for myself. Now, I will never look back. I will always have a therapist in my life.

If you don't have a licensed therapist, start by doing some research. Explore the available therapists in your area and online using the following resources:

- Open Path Collective: openpathcollective.org
- Therapy for Black Girls: therapyforblackgirls.com
- Psychology Today: psychologytoday.com/us

Whose Bags Are You Carrying?

Have you heard the phrase "The body keeps score"? This saying refers to the fact that we carry trauma in our bodies. Trauma therapist Kobe Campbell teaches how pain creates new neural pathways in your brain and changes the DNA structure within your body.[2] This also means trauma can physically pass along to our children. Whose bags are you carrying? You carry the stress of generations in your body. The pain of your mother, grandmother, and generations before them was passed to you without anyone realizing it. The experiences when they were hurt, silenced, or overwhelmed are trapped in your DNA. It's not your fault, Friend, but it is your responsibility. It's up to you to identify the soul injuries in your life and address the pain. You have a responsibility to free your heart so those coming after you can also be free. Some baggage you picked up along the way, but some of the weight was passed down to you. Honor yourself as well as others in your lineage by checking your backpack.

Friend, your backpack is too heavy. Maybe you've lost someone you love, and the grief is suffocating. Maybe you are carrying the pain of a divorce. No one gets married to get divorced, and even

65

if it was the best thing for you, the grief of "what could have been" is heavy. Maybe you know the weight of infertility. You hoped to carry and deliver life for so long that your hope turned bitter. Maybe you've been abused in some way, or your childhood was traumatic. Maybe the pressure to be ten times better has overwhelmed you, and you don't know how to show up as yourself anymore. Maybe you focused so deeply on motherhood when your babies were young you don't know who you are now that they are grown. You secretly feel betrayed now that they have a life outside of you. Maybe you are in the phase of life when your parents need you and no one taught you how to navigate this season.

When was the last time you stopped to investigate your backpack? You continue to carry around all of life's pieces without relief. You cannot heal what you are unwilling to reveal. It is imperative that you take some time to go through your backpack. This will allow you to make intentional decisions about which life lessons you will hold on to and which experiences you need to release. You may not forget what you experienced, but you can choose not to be driven by your pain.

In the next couple of chapters, I will lead you through the steps of checking your baggage. I encourage you to pay attention to your soul as you read. Truly open your invisible backpack and look around. It's time to release the weight.

Do the HeartWork

Take a moment to open your backpack. Use the following one-minute self-coaching activity to begin your work.

 Download the *Disrupting Burnout* journal for a fillable copy of this activity at patricebuckner jackson.com/journal or scan the QR code for access.

*This is a timed activity. The purpose of the timer is to limit your ability to edit your responses. Record exactly what comes to mind.

You will need a notebook, journal, or recording device, and a timer. Give yourself one minute to answer each of the following questions. Do not judge or edit your responses. Document exactly what comes to your heart for each question. Do not allow the recording method to become a barrier. You may write your answer or record yourself answering each question. Use the method that flows easiest for you. Devote the whole minute to one question before you move on to the next. Reset your timer before each question.

Grab your timer, set it to one minute, and begin:

1. What area of your backpack weighs you down the most?
2. What outcome do you desire for that area of your life?
3. What is your ultimate vision for this area of your life?
4. What are the hurdles to accomplishing your vision?
5. What are you afraid of?
6. What are you avoiding?
7. What is one step you can take today to relieve some pressure in this area?

Finally, select a HeartWork partner. Choose someone who you can read this book with and who you trust to challenge you in love and hold you accountable. Use the following questions to set up your partnership.

1. Who can use this message right now for their own life?
2. Who is emotionally positioned to tell you untainted truth with love?
3. Who has the capacity to take this journey with you right now?
4. Who will you accept the challenge from?
5. How often will you check in with your HeartWork partner?
6. What will your check in sessions look like?

Chapter 5

What Is Your Tell?

Friend, how do you know when you are overwhelmed? One of the primary reasons you end up in burnout is because you don't recognize your tell, and typically, you'll have more than one. By tells, I mean your symptoms. Our body, soul, and Spirit tell us when we need to adjust, but we ignore these warnings too often. Symptoms are not the root of the problem, but they are an indication that something is wrong. Your tells are gauges indicating the health of your soul. To disrupt burnout, you must begin to recognize your tells.

My purpose coach, Patrice C. Washington, founder of Seek Wisdom Find Wealth, shared on her podcast, *Redefining Wealth*, that our lives are always speaking to us, but we often fail to listen.[1] Remember, overwhelm is the whisper, but burnout is the demand. We need to heed the whisper to disrupt burnout. You can identify your tells by recognizing how your body, soul, Spirit, relationships, and environment are speaking to you. Let's dive deep into each of these areas. Grab your journal and answer the questions that follow in each section.

Your Body Is Speaking to You

During my "Disrupting Burnout" workshops, women often share how they experience a variety of physical symptoms when they're overwhelmed. These symptoms include the following:

- Tension in the neck and shoulders
- Muscle aches
- Headaches
- Loss of appetite
- Weight gain or loss
- Inability to sleep or difficulty waking up
- Physical exhaustion
- Substance abuse (food, drugs, alcohol, etc.)

In the depths of my burnout experience, my body literally shut down each night without warning. I would work all day, come home, take care of my family, and if I ever dared to sit on the couch or on the side of the bed, I was asleep in the snap of a finger. With no notice and no transition, my body would just shut down. I could not watch a movie or television show. I could not tell my family about my day or hear about theirs. I could fight it if I was on my feet, but if I sat, I was out like a light. I could fall asleep in mid-sentence. When I think of the nights I drove home in this state of exhaustion, it takes my breath away. Thank God for His protection!

My body was speaking to me, but I was not listening. Instead, I normalized this tell. "Of course, I'm tired! I work hard."

What is your physical tell? How does your body speak to you?

Your Soul Is Speaking to You

Burnout is not just a self-care issue. Burnout is a soul-care issue. Pay attention to your soul. When I say "soul," I'm referring to your mind, will, imagination, and emotions. These are the most important indicators of burnout as well as the place where we need to do the work of disrupting burnout. The soul is the bridge between earth and heaven. The soul connects your physical body to your Spirit. The health of your soul determines your connection to Spirit. You should not make decisions based on how you feel because emotions change quickly according to circumstances. However, you should recognize your emotions as a measure of the health of your soul.

How is your soul whispering to you? How is your mental health? Do your daily decisions (your will) align with your purpose? What indications are you receiving from your emotions?

Mind

Have you ever walked into a room and completely forgotten why? Does that happen more often than you want to admit? Forgetfulness is one of the symptoms of overwhelm we often ignore. You may forget tasks or names or simple to-do items. Just like your computer hard drive, human beings have limited mental capacity. Although vast, there is an end to the amount of information our minds can successfully process at any given time. Forgetfulness is a sign we are mentally overloaded and need some free space on our mental hard drive.

At one point, I lost sleep because I was so focused on all the things I forgot to do while at work, and at work, I was distracted by all the things I forgot to do for our home. I never felt like I was in the right place to do the things that needed to be done. According to Rebecca Zucker in the *Harvard Business Review*, some women also experience brain fog, racing thoughts, confusion, or difficulty concentrating when overwhelmed.[2] You may even find it difficult to make decisions or act when your mind is overwhelmed. It's not that you don't have the answer, but you cannot access executive thinking when your mind is tired.

How is your mind speaking to you?

Will

According to Merriam-Webster, your will represents your choices, inclinations, appetites, passions, and determinations.[3] How is your will speaking to you? In burnout, I relinquished several good health habits in exchange for a busy schedule. I ate when I could and whatever I could. I never made time to move my body. The outcome: I gained over one hundred pounds over several years. Friend, you heard me. Over a hundred pounds! And it happened slowly but steadily. In the past, I'd been frustrated with thirty extra pounds. How in the world did I allow it to get so far, you ask? Daily decisions. My will was not in alignment with my purpose. I ate for the moment and not for the future.

How is your will speaking to you? Are your choices and appetites in alignment with where you want to be in your future, or are they holding you to an unfruitful past? It can be as simple as your health decisions, like what you eat or drink. Are you eating and drinking to live a long full life?

Emotions

Amid rock-bottom burnout, I found it almost impossible to control my emotions. Now, let's be honest. I am naturally an emotional creature. If you need someone to cry with you, I'm your girl! Crying is a normal way for me to express myself, so a few tears is not what we're talking about here. The emotions were overwhelming, and I could no longer hold them in. I had held back for so long there was a breach in my emotional levee and the flood had broken through. I found myself in professional meetings unable to hold back the tears. There were days when it was all I could do to get to a bathroom stall so I could cry. I could not explain the emotions and I could not pinpoint the source. I just could not stop crying.

Maybe you're not a crier. Maybe you get what I call "a lil crunchy." A lil crunchy means you're a bit sharper around the edges. You're easily irritated, and everyone around you knows it. Now, Friend, if crunchy is your norm, we need to have a different conversation. However, if you are normally even-keeled or even the opposite of irritable, then you need to pay attention to when you feel irritated and your patience runs short.

Maybe everyday things that wouldn't normally bother you now set you off. Maybe you're not aware of this change, but you notice the people you love seem to need a little distance from you. One thing for sure, if you don't know if you're crunchy, those closest to you can tell you. Pay attention to your family members. If everyone in the house scatters to a different room when you walk in, you might be a lil crunchy, Friend.

How are your emotions speaking to you?

Your Spirit Is Speaking to You

The Spirit is your connection to God. This is the piece of you that remains connected to a world beyond your logic and understanding. This eternal part of your being determines the path for your life on earth and beyond. Monitoring your spiritual health is critical for recognizing overwhelm and burnout.

The word I hear often concerning spiritual disconnection is emptiness. You may be exceptionally successful in your job with a beautiful family and every material thing you need, but if you are not connected to Spirit, you will be empty. Genesis 2:7 states, "Then the LORD God formed the man from the dust of the ground. He breathed the breath of life into the man's nostrils, and the man became a living person."

In the original Hebrew language of the Bible, the word "breath" in this verse means Spirit.[4] When you study this verse in the original language, it means God breathes a living Spirit into the man. He gave us His breath. Don't read that line too fast. The Creator of heaven and earth breathed His life-giving Spirit into man, and *then* the man became a living creature. The man had a body. He was fully equipped, but He was not alive until God breathed into Him. Friend, you are not living until you become aware of the Spirit of

God thriving on the inside of you. Everything you are and everything you were created to be is awakened as you live in His breath.

Remember how I described overwhelm as feeling like you're drowning. You feel the water level of your life rising and you're fighting to hold your head above water. You just need a breath. You just want to breathe. Friend, the Creator of heaven and earth offers you His breath. He created you. He knows everything about you and loves you anyway. He freely offers His breath, His Spirit, His life-giving Spirit to you and to me. Allow yourself to be resuscitated in His presence by seeking Him.

Here is a recipe for reconnecting to His Spirit today. Start with gratitude. Gratefulness changes your perspective and helps you see beyond your present challenge. This may sound like a simple practice, but connecting with gratitude in the midst of overwhelm may prove challenging. Start simply. Walk around your house and look for things you are grateful for, like a family photo, food in the fridge, or the thermostat on the wall. Alternatively, you may choose to think of one person who has had a positive influence on you and send them a "thank you" through direct message or text message. Be sure to tell them why you are thanking them. Finally, walk outside and find three things you appreciate, like a beautiful bird, a flower petal, or fresh air. Honor those blessings by saying, "I am grateful for [insert what you appreciate about your environment]." As you allow yourself to see and appreciate the blessings around you, you will experience the breath of God refilling your spiritual lungs.

Beyond gratitude, recognizing God for who He is through worship also adds perspective and allows you to breathe again. Worship is an act of acknowledging you have been created by the God of this universe for His good pleasure. In worship we recognize the power, prestige, and position of our God. He is not like human beings. "For in him we live and move and exist. "As some of your own poets have said, 'We are his offspring'" (Acts 17:28). He is God and we are His children. We exist in Him. This is majesty and intimacy all at the same time. Worship invites our majestic God into our personal space. We become more aware of Him and He breathes life into us. Without Him, we cannot breathe.

I do not want to take for granted that you have a relationship with Him. I don't know where you're reading these words, but I know our loving Heavenly Father is with you wherever you may be. He knows your heart is overwhelmed and He holds space for you there. You may not be able to explain it to anyone else, but He understands. He knows. He cares. And he loves you.

Here's a prayer to get you started:

Dear Jesus,

I believe in you. I believe you died on the cross, and I believe you were raised from the dead. I believe God gives me breath. I believe you are here with me now. Come into my heart. Be my Lord and my Savior. Forgive my sins and make me new. I desire to be the woman you created me to be, and this is only possible through you. I've tried everything else, and nothing else has satisfied my soul. Make me new and bring your Spirit to life within me. Breathe on me. I need you.

Amen.

WHAT IS YOUR TELL?

Friend, how is your Spirit speaking to you? Are you connected? Are you grateful? Are you abiding with your Heavenly Father? Are you aware of Him? Do you feel connected to your Creator? Are you aware of God's unwavering presence within you? Are you living in alignment with His desires for you?

Your Relationships Are Speaking to You

Busy has a way of disrupting relationships. Just because you are physically near a person does not mean your relationship is healthy. You're likely in the company of your family every day, but are you connecting with them or just running past each other as you move through life? I know you do so much to serve them, but are you loving them in the way they need to be loved? Are they aware of your love?

Remember, burnout is a thief. It comes to steal everything that means the most to you, starting with your most precious relationships. When I was weighed down by burnout, my own child felt like she needed an appointment to spend time with me. While I was so focused on taking care of other people's children in my job, my child felt like she was a hindrance to me. I didn't notice it then, but looking back, I see she tried to stay out of my way because I made my job seem so important. I have lost some friendships and severely fractured others. There are siblings to whom I'm still not close because I was not there for them in the way they needed me. Even as I write to you, I continue working to release shame concerning these fractures in my relationships.

At my speeches and workshops, I always have a receiving line to hug people with tears in their eyes because they resonate with this message. While consoling strangers, I'm aware my own sister is estranged from me, and I allowed this breach to occur. She has no idea how much I love her or how often I think about her. She's not open to receiving that love right now, so I pray, and I wait for another opportunity to make it right. I allowed burnout to rob me of our connection. I take responsibility for that. Think about what you might be allowing burnout and overwhelm to take away from you.

In my travels, I console people who have lost marriages and connections with their children. People are estranged from family members and have lost their best friends due to burnout. Friend, it is difficult to be a good friend when your soul is overwhelmed. One of the things we tend to do when overwhelmed is push people away. We isolate ourselves for fear that someone will see our struggle. We reject the love we need because overwhelm does not allow us to see it as love. It feels like just more to do or someone else who needs something from you when, in reality, you need something from them.

Take a moment to consider your relationships. I'm talking about the ones that matter most to you. Those relationships you want to protect and keep close. At your last breath, you want to look up and see those people around you. Your relationships are speaking to you.

What are your relationships telling you? Are your connections strong? Are you serving out of love or out of obligation? What is the current state of your most precious relationships? Do you have healthy connections with the people you love?

Your Environment Is Speaking to You

Do you watch the show Hoarders? In this reality-based tv show, family and friends work with organizers and counselors to hold an intervention for a person who has buried themself in their home with clutter. I must admit I've never made it through an entire episode because watching the living conditions of the people on the show increases anxiety for me. I don't understand how any person could live like that because that kind of life is not logical. Clutter is never about the clutter itself. It's never as simple as just cleaning up. I'm convinced the experts can clean the mess, but it will soon return if the root of the hoarding is never addressed.

One of the primary signs of overwhelm is clutter and chaos. Your environment is a physical manifestation of your soul. If you have clutter and disorder in your physical space, you likely have clutter and disorder in your mind, will, and emotions. Remember those stacks of papers under my desk in that otherwise beautiful office? I never allowed anyone behind my desk. I met with students and staff members at a table in front of my desk and then returned to the paper monsoon to get my work done. It's no wonder I struggled to keep deadlines and complete projects. How in the world did I expect to be productive like that? Every now and then, I would just have enough and take a day or two to sort, shred, and file. However, because I was unaware of the root of the problem, the monsoon eventually returned.

The tells in your environment are not limited to physical clutter. Sometimes you may find yourself in an emotionally toxic environment. Continuing to exist in a space where you feel criticized and demoralized is a sign of burnout. Healthy environments may challenge you, but the challenge pushes you toward purpose and peace. When your environment distracts you from your destiny and tears away at your dignity, it's time to make a change.

Check your environment, Friend. How is your physical space? How about your emotional space? Does your environment promote the best in you or is it an indication of a weary soul?

What is your tell? What are the ways your body, soul, Spirit, relationships, and environment attempt to get your attention? Friend, the evidence is in you and all around you. God created us with automatic warning mechanisms so we will stop and take notice. Every symptom is significant. Disrupting burnout is not about living perfectly after reading this book; disrupting burnout is about becoming so self-aware that you never miss another sign.

> *Disrupting burnout is not about living perfectly after reading this book; disrupting burnout is about becoming so self-aware that you never miss another sign.*

Do the HeartWork

If you haven't taken time to answer the questions in this chapter yet, go back and identify your tells by writing out your answers, Friend. This work is essential to your process of disrupting burnout.

 Download the *Disrupting Burnout* journal for a fillable copy of this activity at patricebuck-nerjackson.com/journal or scan the QR code for access.

Chapter 6

Check Your Baggage

In this chapter, we'll explore sections of your backpack that keep you stuck in the Cycle of Burnout. Imagine you're cleaning out your backpack, preparing for a big trip. Visualize yourself taking the bag from your back. Sit on the floor in a comfortable position with the bag in front of you. Unzip the largest compartment and peak inside. Begin taking each experience, idea, thought, system, and belief out of your bag. Now, imagine yourself with an empty bag and all your things sitting on the floor around you.

I'm going to ask you a series of questions. Take your time to read the section, understand each question and search through your baggage for your answer. Write your response to each question in your *Disrupting Burnout* journal. Take your time; there is no time limit here. Remember there is no right or wrong answer to any of these questions. Your truth is your truth. Our goal here is just to face it for what it is and decide if it should remain in your backpack. It's time to acknowledge what you've been carrying.

What Is Your Definition of Work?

I grew up in Crocketville, a small settlement in Hampton County in the Lowcountry of South Carolina. Imagine a rural family farm with dirt roads, cornfields, family gatherings, and air so pure you can smell an incoming rain shower. In Crocketville, work was not just income; work was survival. Work was waking up before the sun each morning to take care of the animals and go to the fields, not to return until the sun went down again. Work was back-breaking, sweat-inducing labor.

My brother and cousins rode off in the wee hours of summer mornings to the watermelon fields with my Granddaddy Joe. They would form a line across the field, pick the ripe watermelons, and toss them, one by one, person to person, until they filled a large hauling truck. My grandaddy then drove the truck to the farmer's market on Saturdays to sell the watermelons. I walked through fields of corn, beans, peas, and okra with my sister and Grandma Senie Mae, filling bushel baskets to be sold or given to friends and family. My stepdad worked twelve-hour shifts as a security guard, only to come home to work the fields on the weekends. My mother opened a local hair salon, where she took her first client at six in the morning and the last at eight o'clock at night every day except Sunday and Monday. Monday was the national hairdresser's day off since they work so hard on Saturdays, and Sunday was for the Lord. I sat in that shop so many days, folding shampoo towels after they were washed and dried, sanitizing combs and brushes, or sweeping hair after Mama gave somebody a new haircut. In Crocketville, work was an unending sacrifice. You worked when you were tired. You worked when you were sick. You never complained because work was survival.

Without noticing, I took this definition of work to the university setting. As a young professional, I had to be the first person to arrive each morning and the last to leave. I literally watched the cars to make sure none of my co-workers beat me to the office. I had to be the one to turn the lights on. I wouldn't dare allow my boss to get to work before me. *What would they think of my work ethic?* I said yes too often, took on too many projects, and attended as many student programs as I could. I woke up checking my email and went to sleep at night doing the same. I was on call for campus crises almost twenty-four-seven and remained available even when I wasn't on call.

I wasn't tossing watermelons, but you couldn't tell my heart that. In my mind, doing a good job at work meant working until I couldn't work anymore. I drove myself to burnout. Who was I to complain? My people were still in the fields of Crocketville. How dare I admit to being tired when I worked in a cushy air-conditioned office. I was no longer in Crocketville, but I brought Crocketville to campus with me. Crocketville was in me, and it almost ruined me.

Now, hear me, Friend. There is nothing wrong with Crocketville. I am so grateful for my upbringing. The foundations of community, work ethic, and faith from my hometown served me well in my life. I have experienced success and accomplished much based on those foundations. I was rewarded with promotions due to my work ethic. However, the definition of work I learned in Crocketville no longer aligns with who I am. I was raised in Crocketville, but I am no longer in Crocketville. My upbringing defined how I approached life and work, but that definition was not in alignment with who God created me to be today. Crocketville was in my backpack, and I had to determine how I would like to carry it.

We all have our own version of what we think work should look like. Maybe you find yourself overworking, trying to chase a standard of worthiness created in your family. Maybe you find yourself overcommitted because you learned every minute of your day should be full. Maybe you cannot say no to church obligations because you learned your level of holiness is based on your level of self-sacrifice. Maybe you learned nobility is serving your community even at the cost of your own health and wellbeing.

What have you learned about work that is negatively impacting your life right now?

I met a woman at a new teacher workshop in Savannah, Georgia, who shared that her father was the doctor in a very small town when she was growing up. She described how he worked long hours, seven days every week, and how his off time was often interrupted by medical emergencies. She was impacted by her father's work ethic and the admiration he received from the community so much that she found herself being just like him. She worked tirelessly to serve her students and their families. She stayed after school and even went into after-school care to serve the students in her class. She had experiences where she had to find someone to take care of her children while she was taking care of the children in her class after hours.

This woman realized the negative impact her work definition was having on her family and took steps to change this pattern before it was too late. She was so desperate to change her definition of work that she and her family decided to move to Savannah for a fresh start. What is your definition of work and where did you learn it? How has that definition impacted your life? What changes do you need to make to your work standards, Friend?

What Is Your Vice?

What do you run to for comfort? What person, place, or thing creates the illusion of peace for you? It's difficult to see what you are running from until you acknowledge what you are running to. Yours might not be a typical vice. When you think of a vice, your mind may go to drugs, sex, or alcohol. Those intoxicants may very well be real struggles for some women, but I'd like to add a few we don't often discuss.

As accomplished women, we often run to information for comfort. Doreen Rainey, the RADICAL Success Coach, calls this phenomenon "information gathering." I must admit the first time I heard Doreen explain this vice, I was quite offended. I consider myself a learned woman, and learning has always been a place of safety for me. When I don't know what else to do, I know I can learn something, read something, consume something. The problem with gathering more information, as Doreen explains it, is simply learning makes us feel accomplished, so we never do anything with the information we gather. Therefore, we see no transformation. The learning becomes a false indicator of success when there has been no progress.

Maybe when you're stressed, you reach for another book, podcast, or personal development video, but you never implemented what you learned in the last one. Accomplished women get stuck in cycles of learning without taking action. Learning becomes a crutch because we believe we are making progress. Really, we are just filling ourselves to a sort of intellectual obesity with no forward movement. Learning in and of itself is not a bad thing, but when you use learning to compensate for a soul injury, you overload your backpack.

We also need to discuss relying on the advice of others as a vice. As with information overload, you seek a coach, mentor, or guru to give you a magic, abracadabra resolution so you can feel better in the moment, but this is not true healing. One of the beautiful things that came out of the pandemic was so many more people sharing their knowledge and expertise through social media. This was also one of the most dangerous outcomes of the pandemic as there is no vetting process for these self-proclaimed experts. Anyone with a cell phone has access to share with the world, and in our desperation, we consume all this content. You find yourself at a stuck place and you just want out. You're willing to listen to anyone who seems to have an answer.

Friend, I believe in finding the right coach. I have seen the impact of listening to the right people in my own life. I have also seen the consequences of listening to someone else without hearing my own Spirit first. Holy Spirit speaks to me about me, but sometimes I ignore Him and resort to an answer from a human I can see. What worked for someone else may not be your answer. On this journey, you will learn how to hear what God is speaking to your heart so you don't waste time following a path set out for someone else. Learn to trust yourself. Your answer is inside of you.

Finally, I need you to consider how achievement might be a vice for you. Anytime you hear sage advice more than once in a lifetime, you need to hold on to it. One piece of advice has kept me grounded through the years, and I've heard it from two powerful women. At a university

"You can have it all, but not all at the same time."

where I worked, we held an annual leadership lecture series. Through these lectures, I had the honor of meeting Dr. Cornel West, Soledad

O'Brien, Condoleezza Rice, and Nikki Giovanni, just to name a few. During these events, the distinguished guests had dinner with a small group of students and administrators prior to addressing a large crowd of community members.

On two occasions, several years apart, we hosted former Secretary of State Madeleine Albright and former First Lady Laura Bush. Both women were asked the question: How do you balance it all? (Side note: It's interesting that, in my years of attending these events, no one asked the male guests how they balanced it all, but I digress.) Both women gave the same answer: "You can have it all, but not all at the same time." The former First Lady shared how when her daughters were young, she took a back seat on community initiatives and projects, dedicating herself to caring for her babies. As they grew older, she gained more freedom to invest her time outside of her home. She encouraged the crowd of college students to honor the season you're in and expect that season to change, which means your priorities will change.

This advice has carried me through the different seasons of my life. When I was that young, single professional, I made ten-year plans and mapped out exactly where I would be and what I would achieve at each junction. Life has a way of teaching you to calm down. Now, I have no list. I learned to seize the moment. I give my very best in the season I am living in, within the boundaries of what my life allows. I'm learning that comparison is a thief, so I walk my own journey and keep my eyes off everyone else's. I learned to be content while pressing. I know how to work without striving. I don't always do it well, but what peace I experience when I do.

Be fair to your dreams. Purpose is a process, not a pinnacle you arrive at someday. There is no destiny you can microwave for five minutes, let sit for one, and enjoy. Our culture of going viral has ruined the concept of consistency. We forget that the people who "go viral" were usually grinding in the shadows for years before anyone noticed. Some of my favorite influencers have hundreds of thousands of followers, but they'd been pressing for ten years or more before hitting that number. Slow and steady win the race every time. Stop trying to get the quick win and give steady and consistent a try. Dreams take time to mature. Destiny takes time to develop. Invest well where you are today, and you will be more than ready when the next door opens.

What vices do you run to for comfort? Where do you hide when you're overwhelmed? What habits and behaviors hold you captive to old belief systems?

What Do You Believe about God's Thoughts about You?

Recently, I had the opportunity to encourage another woman concerning God's love for her. I told her how God loved her before she could love Him back. I shared how He pursued her until she was ready to accept His love. I told her He was not angry with her, and He was ecstatic that she would invite Him into her heart. It was a beautiful conversation, and I could feel Holy Spirit's presence as we shared.

Immediately after the conversation, as I sat for a moment, just reflecting, I heard a question in my heart: "PBJ, do you believe that about you? Do you believe I love you like that?" The question came as a shock because, at that moment, I could not say yes. I wanted to answer affirmatively, but the truth was I had never considered His love for me in this way. I'd had similar conversations with many people over the years, but never with myself.

I grew up in a very religious environment. We went to church at least three to four times every week and church services lasted three to four hours. The church was the center of our lives; everything was planned around the church schedule. I am so grateful for my upbringing because it's the foundation of who I am today, but I didn't learn much about God's love. I learned of His wrath, of His holiness, how we should honor Him, and how we should fear Him. I learned heaven is the goal and hell is to be avoided at all costs. I learned to walk on eggshells and to hide from Him in shame when I missed the mark. I accepted a God who I believed was waiting to punish me if I made any missteps. This was not the God I presented to others, but if I'm honest, this angry God with a chip on His shoulder was the God I tried to serve up until the year I wrote this book. I always saw Him as my Heavenly Father, but Father to me meant disengaged, separate, and harsh. Father, in my mind, was someone I needed to impress to receive His love, but who was not easily impressed. Father was a high, lofty position my heart desired to touch, but respect kept me far from Him.

I am learning, even in this moment, that our Heavenly Father is not like earthly fathers. Through study of His Word, I'm learning His heart is to love first. In Romans 5:8 (NIV), Paul wrote, "But God demonstrates his own love for us in this: While we were still sinners, Christ died for us." God gave me His very best and paid the ultimate price to have a relationship with me before I could ever do anything good or bad. "For this is how God loved the world: He gave his one and only Son, so that everyone who believes in him will not perish but have eternal life" (John 3:16). And in Exodus 20:6, God says, "But I lavish unfailing love for a thousand generations on those who love me and obey my commands." My Heavenly Father is not like man. He is the only one who can love with an unfailing love.

I am also learning He didn't just love the world, but He also loves me personally and specifically. God loves me so specifically that He has counted every hair on my head (Luke 12:7). He tracks my sorrows, stores my tears in a bottle in heaven, and records each one in a heavenly book (Psalm 56:8). How intimate is that kind of love! I am learning that the Creator of heaven and earth is madly in love with me, and it is safe for me to love Him.

What do you believe about God's thoughts concerning you?

What Are You Hiding?

During a virtual keynote speech, a participant asked me if I carry shame connected with my burnout story. I appreciated the question because releasing shame is an ongoing process for me. I told her, "Yes, I have shame attached to how I left my job with no notice, but the more I tell the story the more I'm released from the shame." I can acknowledge that I disappointed many people in that transition *and* it was the best decision I could make for me at that moment. I embrace both truths.

Who do you believe you are? Shame attaches itself to your identity and holds on like a leech sucking away your strength. Shame will hold you captive to one season of your life when time is steadily moving on. Shame will cause you to hide instead of allowing your brilliance to shine through. Shame is the first negative emotion mentioned in the Bible.

Genesis 3:7-8 says:

> At that moment their eyes were opened, and they suddenly felt shame at their nakedness. So they sewed fig leaves together to cover themselves. When the cool evening breezes were blowing, the man and his wife heard the Lord God walking about in the garden. So they hid from the Lord God among the trees.

And the response to shame is always the same. We hide. We hide our gifts. We hide our accomplishments. We hide our brilliance. I've learned shame can only thrive in places we are willing to hide. Shame cannot live where we shine the light. I am determined to tell my whole story, spreading light into every corner of my life so shame has no place to hide. You too can tell your story. It's the only way to release the grip of shame.

Shame and brilliance cannot thrive in the same space, so it's time to walk out of shame and into the fullness of brilliance. Uncover what you believe you need to hide. Say it out loud. Tell a trusted friend or mentor. Speak with a counselor. Say that thing you think no one can see so you can be free.

What are you hiding? Where do you need to shine light on your story to uncover experiences that are holding you back?

Who Do You Need to Forgive?

Growing up, I felt abandoned by my biological father. I heard stories of how he deserted my mother and me after he found out she was pregnant. I rarely saw him because he was in the Army and always lived far away. This distance solidified our estrangement in my mind. He was married and had more children. I was jealous of them because I felt like they got what belonged to me. I grew up with a hate in my heart for him, which led to me hating every part of me that looked like him. Although I can look back now and see his attempts to connect with me, I rejected every attempt in my effort to protect my heart.

I will never forget the season when God began to deal with my heart concerning my father. I was a young adult living in San Antonio, Texas, and connected to a powerful church. I was on fire for God! I was excited about my walk with Him and willing to do whatever He said—until He said, "I want you to forgive your father."

Uhm, wait a minute, God. Isn't there a ministry you want me to do or some hungry people I can feed? God asked for the one thing I was not ready to give Him, my bitterness. I held unforgiveness for my father so long that bitterness began taking root in my heart.

Hebrews 12:15 instructs us to avoid bitterness:

> Look after each other so that none of you fails to receive the grace of God. Watch out that no poisonous root of bitterness grows up to trouble you, corrupting many.

Before God would allow my brilliance to truly flow, He required me to offer Him my heart so He could heal it. Notice I said, *God did the healing*. This wasn't something I could do on my own. I needed the love and power of Almighty God to release this pain. And He did! Today, my father is my best friend. It took time and lots of prayer, but we now enjoy the relationship we should have had from the beginning. I am a Daddy's girl! Folks who meet us now have no idea of the journey we've taken. There is no residue of unforgiveness or bitterness left between us.

The direction of my life completely shifted after I allowed God to pull up the bitter roots. I met my husband. I got promoted several times at work. I discovered my brilliance and took the leap to live fully in it. The freedom I experience today began the day I decided to allow God to help me forgive. If you want to hear Dad and me tell the whole story, listen to episodes 9 and 10 of the *Disrupting Burnout* podcast.[1][2]

I hear you saying, "They don't deserve it." I know, but remember forgiveness is not for them. Forgiveness is for you. Bitterness will take root in your heart and strangle the life out of every dream. You deserve to live free. You were created to live free. Jesus died so you can be free. You didn't deserve the sacrifice of Jesus either, but He gave his life out of love. Holding on to unforgiveness will skew your vision and bring calamity. Remember the root determines the fruit. You do not want a harvest of bitter fruit. Allow God to pull up the bitter roots and replace them with the fruit of His Spirit. This is true freedom.

Friend, who hurt you? Who do you need to forgive? How did they hurt you? What exactly do you need to forgive them for?

Recently, God showed me I had a root of bitterness in my heart against Him. To make His point, He took me back to my childhood, when I was the little girl who carried her doll everywhere. At the age of four, I had a whole diaper bag full of tiny diapers and fake baby bottles with disappearing liquid. If you asked me what I wanted to be when I grew up, I would have said a mommy. When I got married, I just knew my dreams were coming true. I love my BabyGirl, my daughter from my husband's first marriage, but my heart ached for a child from my own womb. BabyGirl is her own miracle, not a replacement for the baby I desired. Looking at a picture of us together, many people have a hard time telling us apart even though we share no blood between us. She is a miracle in her own right, but not the miracle I expected.

My husband is the last male in his direct family line, so I expected God would bless us with a son to carry on the Jackson name. I just knew this little baby was coming in one year. Two years. Three years. Four years. Five years. No baby. I took a pregnancy test every month. Eventually, I was diagnosed with polycystic ovarian syndrome (PCOS), a symptom of which is irregular cycles. In those years, I could go several months to a year without having a period at all. So I took pregnancy tests every month, in secret, in the bathroom by myself. I took them in secret because I didn't want to drive Edward crazy, and I didn't want to look crazy to anyone else. They were negative every month.

At one point, we thought maybe we were called to foster or adopt. When the caseworker visited our home, she sat with us and walked us through some of the process. During her visit, I became uneasy to the point that I had to walk away. I knew in my Spirit that adoption just wasn't right for us. I couldn't explain it. I don't have an explanation to this day, but I knew it wasn't the route for us. So we stopped that process and never revisited it. And years continued to go by.

The Bible says hope deferred makes the heart sick, and every year without a baby broke my heart (Proverbs 13:12). After eight years of praying, hoping, and trying, I decided I could not believe anymore. I accepted my fate as an infertile woman and went on to throw my energy into work and ministry. I thought I'd let it go at that point. Mother's Day was still a hard day, but at least I wasn't praying over negative pregnancy tests every month. I felt better. I felt like I could breathe. I could laugh again. I moved on with my life, or so I thought.

I hit a point where I felt distant from God, like I couldn't hear Him or feel Him like I used to. Through prayer and therapy, I realized my heart was still broken from never having a baby. I was full of disappointment. I'd released the dream, but I'd never mourned. I'd accepted what seemed to be God's will, but I had never healed. In truth, I was angry with Him. I watched women who professed to never want children have them while I was left barren.

As soon as this bitterness came to my attention, I began to confess my anger to God and He began to heal this area of life. Mother's Day is still hard, and even writing this section brings tears to my eyes, but I am no longer angry. When I have moments of sadness, I feel Him embrace me with love as I release the tears. I walk this journey with God, trusting that He knows what's best for me and He holds my heart when I want to fall apart. He understands.

Are you holding a grudge against God? Do you harbor any disappointment about the way your life has unfolded? Do you have any bitterness concerning what God allowed or did not allow in your life?

You can confess pain and resentment to Him. He can handle it. Maybe you endured childhood trauma, or maybe he didn't allow you to go into the career field you desired. Maybe you experienced divorce or endured illness. Maybe you lost a loved one or survived abuse. Whatever bitterness you may be holding in your heart, it is safe for you to confess it to Him.

Tell Him you're angry. Let Him know your heart is broken. His shoulders are strong enough to handle your bitterness, but your heart is not strong enough to continue to carry it. God is faithful, and He is loving to forgive you and to heal those places where you hold bitterness. Even when the bitterness is against Him, He is kind and loving toward you. In fact, He is already aware of the bitterness. Your confession is just an invitation for Him to heal it.

What Are Your Blind Spots?

In my first breakthrough in counseling, I shared how I felt like I was disappointing everyone in my life. I didn't feel like I was a good wife, mom, daughter, sister, or auntie. The only area I felt like I excelled was my career. My therapist pointed out how I limited my access to receiving love to what I could do for other people. She called it transactional love. I didn't feel like I was a good wife, mom, daughter, sister, or auntie because I didn't feel like I could give my people everything they needed from me. She helped me see how I evaluated my worthiness based on what I could give. I couldn't see this for myself. It just seemed normal to me, so normal that I couldn't see it as a barrier. My therapist offered me a mirror to see this blind spot in my life so I could address it.

You cannot see your blind spots because they feel natural to you. Some of the ideas, beliefs, and systems holding you back have become impossible for you to see. In the HeartWork Community, my virtual coaching community, we reveal the blind spots in our lives. I often have the opportunity to hold up a mirror with participants to help them see the full story. Understanding the source of false narratives empowers you to dismantle that story and create a new belief in that area of your life. Allow someone to help you. Look in the mirror so you can see what you are truly carrying.

What blind spots are hindering your brilliance?

Do the Heart Work

What does the Bible say about God's thoughts about you? Search the scriptures to find evidence of how much God loves you. Select three verses that speak to you in the most powerful way. Write these verses on an index card and carry them around with you through the day. Read your verses aloud to yourself several times throughout each day until you can say them without reading.

Chapter 7

Change the Narrative

The most critical part of checking your baggage is identifying and revising the stories you tell yourself. Prior to my burnout moment, I told myself no one would care for my students like I did. I called all 25,000 students "mine" because that was the way I saw them. I saw myself in this pseudo-parental role and I wore it like a badge of honor. Some of my students even called me "Mama Dean" to add the parental role to my professional title, dean of students. I loved them like they were mine and at times blurred the lines in my heart, failing to acknowledge they were not mine. The worst part of leaving my executive position was leaving my students. Some of them had allowed me to walk through the deepest traumas with them. I'd held their hands and held them close when needed. I'd listened to their troubles and guided them through as they allowed. What would they do without me?

Well, I'll tell you what they did without me. They kept living. They kept breathing. They even had the nerve to graduate and pursue careers without me being there. The nerve of them to survive without me! I say that in jest now, but there was a time when I truly thought they wouldn't be okay without me. Friend, I told myself I couldn't take time off, change jobs, or even take a break during the day because my students needed me. It wasn't until I could not be there due to burnout that I realized this story I'd told myself was not true. I'd had a powerful impact on their lives, and they could make it without me. More than one thing can be true.

What Story Are You Telling Yourself?

Human beings are natural storytellers. Whether recounting the story of a first love or passing down family traditions, our stories are our lives. For as long as human beings have existed, we've shared stories as a cornerstone of communication. We tell stories naturally even to ourselves; our brains work that way. Think of the mama trying to get in touch with her teenager who won't answer the phone. Often, the mother's mind wanders to a worst-case scenario. There have been too many days when I pictured my child in a ditch somewhere just because I couldn't reach her. Anytime there's a lack of information, human beings fill in that gap with our imagination. And most of the time, the story we create is much worse than reality.

Identify the Gaps

To beat burnout and live in brilliance, you must take control of the stories you are telling yourself. The first step in controlling your story is to identify where you have a lack of information and you've filled in the gaps with your imagination. You may find gaps in your assumptions about the emotions or motives of other people. There are often gaps concerning the outcome of a specific action or decision. You have gaps concerning your future, the decisions of others, your health, the world, and so much more. As intelligent as you are, you cannot know everything. So, Friend, learn to accept the fact that you have gaps in information. Stop forcing yourself to have an answer when you don't. Learn to rest in the unknown.

Identify the Stories

Next, you must identify the stories you've created as well as those passed along to you. What stories are you telling yourself? What stories have you created in your mind and in your heart that are leading you to burnout? What stories did you learn from others?

I told myself stories like:

- I need to work ten times harder than my colleagues.
- A good Christian sacrifices everything.
- God is fed up with me.
- The next promotion (or degree) will make me happy and bring me peace.
- If I don't do it, nobody else will.
- If I don't show up, no one will help my students.
- I must have a sparkling house and a great dinner ready. Otherwise, I'm not a good wife.

- If I don't answer the phone, the person calling won't love me anymore. Worse, they'll think I don't love them.
- If I don't respond to every text message, people will think I don't care.
- If I don't go above and beyond at work, no one will respect me.
- If I don't say yes to every project, my boss will think I'm not committed.
- If I don't say yes to every church obligation, people will think I don't love Jesus.

How many of these stories resonate with you? Have you told similar stories? Did you learn similar stories? It can be most difficult to change a story when some element of it is true. It may be true that no one else will show up if you don't, but does that mean you have to? It may be true that your people feel unloved when you don't respond in the way they desire, but does that mean what they feel is true? Are you allowing yourself to be tangled up in their story of not being loved?

Friend, you must question the stories you carry and confront them with the truth because the stories you believe create your reality. My stories were strangling me. They were choking the life out of me.

Identify your stories by answering the following questions in your *Disrupting Burnout* journal:

- What stories are you telling yourself?
- What story have you created, in your own heart, that's leading you to burnout and choking the life out of you?

Apply Truth

After you identify the story, you must apply truth to that story. Now, this can be uncomfortable because the truth doesn't always feel good. However, Jesus taught the truth you believe will make you free (John 8:32). In my case, I believed everyone in my life needed me. The truth was it was less about people needing me and more about my emotional need to be needed. It was more about my identity being wrapped up in achievement. It was more about my self-worth being wrapped up in validation from others. That truth is still tough to swallow. My truth is I'm very good at supporting people in their toughest times, *and* I take it overboard if I do not honor my boundaries.

Apply truth by answering the following questions in your *Disrupting Burnout* journal:

- What is the truth concerning your stories?
- What is the truth from the Word of God?

I love Tabitha Brown. Before she became a vegan expert, America's Auntie, and a social media influencer, Tabitha Brown tried to be what she believed Hollywood and the professional world expected her to be. In an interview on *The Sister Circle Podcast* with Chrystal Evans Hurst called "Showing Up for Yourself," Tabitha described how she straightened her hair, tried to hide her North Carolina accent, and told herself the story that in order to be accepted and successful, she had to be what "they" wanted her to be. "They" refers to whomever held her next big break. It wasn't until Tabitha made the decision to be genuine and honest with herself that she created her own platform and her life completely changed. Everything she'd waited more than twenty years for immediately flooded into her life when she confronted her stories with the truth.

Sometimes your stories come from those who should love you most. My client, Camila, immigrated to the United States when she was a child. Camila had to learn a new language and new culture. Then, in her high school years, her family told her it was time to leave school so she could help bring in some money for the family. Camila begged to stay in school as she believed this was the key to a better life. She even had teachers speak to her family on her behalf in hopes her parents would change their minds, but that plan failed.

Eventually, Camila made a hard decision. She moved out of her parents' home and moved in with the family of a friend to stay in school. This powerhouse of a woman was so dedicated to her education that she went from high school diploma straight through to her doctorate degree with no breaks. Dr. Camila didn't quit school until she had obtained a terminal degree. As we laud this great accomplishment, we also need to acknowledge the stories sown into Camilla along the way.

People told Camilla stories like these:

- You're abandoning your family.
- We worked so hard to bring you here, and now you turn your back on us.
- You think you're better than us.

These stories plagued Camila into adulthood, marriage, motherhood, and professional life. As accomplished as she was, she could not see her own value. She felt the need to apologize for everything and shied away from advocating for herself. After joining The W.E.L., my community for women who lead in education, Camila gained confidence. Having other accomplished women applaud her, support her, and challenge her gave Camila the strength she needed to begin a job search for her next position. She saw the positive impact she had on students like her and felt called to make that impact at a higher level. Through supportive community and reframing her stories, Camila recognized and accepted her own brilliance.

If you did not do so while reading this section, now is the time to do this HeartWork. Write down some of the stories you carry. Under each story, identify the truth you know about each situation. Remember you do not have to fill in the gaps. You can learn to accept that you don't know it all. This activity may be a challenge, so show yourself some grace.

Here's some truth to get you started:

- The truth is you are worthy. No matter how hard you work, you were created worthy.
- The truth is you are not in competition with the next woman or any other person. God created you with your very own innate, unique brilliance. There is no competition when you show up as you.
- When you live in that brilliance, not only is there ease and grace, but there's also power and impact.
- The truth is you are valuable.
- The truth is you are loved by our Heavenly Father regardless of your works, and there is nothing you can do to separate yourself from His love.

Change the Narrative

To be free, you must apply the truth to the stories you're telling yourself. After you apply the truth, change the narrative. Speak to yourself in a different way. You must cast down stories that come to mind as soon as they come up. This is important. Speak the truth out loud to yourself. Truth is activated when it's spoken. The more you speak that truth, the more freedom you will experience in your heart, your mind, your Spirit, and your body. So if you're ready to disrupt burnout and embrace brilliance, Friend, it's time to speak the truth. Let's start here:

Declare this aloud: "I align my life with the plan of God for me. I release everything that hinders my progress, and I embrace everything that leads to brilliance. I am healthy, wealthy, strong, and courageous. I will identify every mindset that does not align with my Heavenly Father's thoughts about me and replace it with His design. I see me as God sees me."

I want to encourage your heart, Friend. You can be free. In our foundational scripture, Jesus said, "My yoke is easy, and my burden is light" (Matthew 11:30). If your responsibilities are heavy and choking you or your burden is too much for you to bear, it's not something God gave you. That's the truth.

Head, Heart, Hands

It's often said, "If you know better, you do better." Friend, I'm here to tell you that isn't true. Raise your hand if there's something you know right now that you haven't implemented in your life. I'm raising both hands because I'm the queen of gathering new knowledge and doing nothing with it. Before we move on to building boundaries, we need to discuss the power of belief. Changing the narrative requires you to transform your belief systems.

This journey is not just about new knowledge. You know enough right now to live in freedom. The problem is you don't know how to apply what you know. In disrupting burnout, we transform knowledge into action. You will be a different woman at the end of this experience because you'll know how to apply the strategies. The path to transformation begins in your head, moves to your heart, and results in your hands.

Head

Your head represents awareness. All transformation begins with access and awareness. People often think money causes the great divide among people in our society; I would argue access and awareness are the real chasms. You cannot implement what you don't know. It's difficult to imitate what you have never seen.

I've seen the power of awareness in my own life. Joining coaching communities with women who are accomplishing goals I set for myself gave me a view of what was possible for me. I'm living in circumstances I couldn't have dreamed up just a few short months ago because I've been exposed to more. And, Friend, let me tell you! Once you've been exposed, it becomes difficult, torturous even, to settle for less. Awareness provokes you to consider new possibilities, but don't stop at awareness. Alone, it's not enough to produce lasting change. The next step is critical.

Heart

The heart stands for belief, and belief is the core component of transformation. We feel proud of ourselves when we gain new knowledge, insight, or awareness, but if you're honest, you know awareness is not enough. You have sufficient knowledge right now to move mountains. Knowledge is not your problem; your lack of belief in what you know is the problem. Even deeper, not believing it's true for you is the real problem. It's often easier to think powerful thoughts about others than it is to accept the same power for yourself. You can learn something new every day of the week, but it means nothing if you do not believe it. You don't get what you know; you get what you believe.

Have you ever considered why affirmations are so powerful? Affirmations work because the act of speaking creates belief. Your words are powerful creators. Speaking according to your awareness moves knowledge from your head to your heart. Awareness becomes belief through confession. I would take the leap to say if you look at your life right now, you will see you are living in the results of what you have said over and over. If you want to start believing something new, begin to say something new. Say it before you believe it. Say it until you believe it.

Sometimes we need to borrow belief until we have it for ourselves. Prior to writing this book, I often said, "I'm not a writer." I was never heralded as a good writer in school. My writing was always returned to me with more red markings than black type. I didn't become a reader until I started writing a dissertation and one of my professors told me reading would make me a better writer (this is true by the way). I wrote an entire dissertation based on borrowed belief. The leader of my dissertation committee, Dr.

Teri Melton, believed in my ability to finish, so I trusted her. Dr. Melton had years of research experience under her belt as well as hundreds of students she had supported through the dissertation process. I believed more in her than I believed in myself, so I just did what she told me to do. My belief in my writing ability did not change in that process. I graduated with my doctorate still saying, "I'm not a writer," but I graduated because I had someone in my life who believed when I did not.

This book you are reading right now is evidence that borrowed belief produces fruit. I almost did not write this book. My dissertation process was so traumatizing I was convinced I never wanted to write again. Now, let me be clear because I know there are some real PhD horror stories out there. My dissertation committee was the best. I would not have finished without their support. However, the dissertation process is not set up to be empowering. Defending your work in that process feels like hazing, like being intellectually jumped into the Academy. Therefore, many people quit before accomplishing the goal. Others finish but carry the scars of the process for years to come.

The trauma of the dissertation process kept me from beginning this book project for several years. I was very comfortable speaking but was unwilling to even start writing. I believed writing was not my ministry, and I lived in that belief until I met a book coach named Candice L. Davis. Candice challenged the belief that I am not a writer. She confronted me with the conflict of how I could possibly be a great speaker and not a be great writer. She shared that writing and speaking are truly the same gift; it's all communication. I had never considered it that way before. Candice invited me into writing sessions where I could write along with others who were writing for the first time and some who had published several works. She had me join monthly meetings where we discussed our writing challenges and celebrated each other's victories. Candice addressed my fears with logic and challenged my story about myself. As I typed more words into this manuscript, I was forced to acknowledge I was doing exactly what I always said I could not do. The proof was in front of me, and I could no longer deny it. I was writing.

I am a writer. I will need an editor, but I am a writer. I became anxious about sharing this work at some points, but I am a writer. I was never praised or awarded for my writing before, but I am a writer. This book is proof. Borrowed belief will carry you until you begin to believe for yourself.

Let me be clear, Friend. HeartWork is not about following your heart; that idea does not align with the Word of God. HeartWork is about transforming your heart. You need to believe something different to live a different life. Speak to your heart until you begin to believe the truth about your brilliance. Confess the truth in a whisper or in a roar. The volume does not matter, but

You will have whatever you say, and you will be what you believe.

the repetition is important. Say it more than once. Say it every day. Say it before you believe it. Say it until the burden falls from your shoulders. Say it until your heart is free. Take the awareness you receive in these pages and say it from your lips. Then watch what happens as your heart begins to believe in your brilliance. At the core of our conversation here are your belief systems. You will have whatever you say, and you will be what you believe. The HeartWork strategies will help you speak and believe the truth. After doing your own HeartWork, powerful action just flows naturally.

Hands

Finally, the hands represent action. You will always act according to what you believe. Most people try to move directly from awareness to action. Then they experience shame when that cycle doesn't work. You are not lazy or unintelligent. Change is not about motivation because motivation is fleeting. Change only occurs when your beliefs align with your awareness. Change the narrative to change your behavior. Become open to new awareness, confess the truth until you believe it, and watch how your actions begin to align. The doing becomes easier and more authentic when you honor the path.

Do the HeartWork

As an accomplished woman, I know you've been in many environments that led you to create stories of perfectionism, overcompensating, and imposter syndrome. It is critical to your purpose that you rewrite these stories.

Here are a few affirmations from the women in my HeartWork Community to help you get started:

- I am proud of myself.
- I positively impact everyone I encounter.
- I am beautifully created by God.
- I speak with grace and power. My voice commands attention.
- I am enough, right now, as I am today.
- I am a Woman of God.
- I am fearfully and wonderfully made by God. (Psalm 139:14)
- I am loved no matter what.
- I am worthy without performance or accomplishment.
- I live in peace. I operate from a place of peace. Peace is my portion.
- I was born to shine.
- I always win.

Begin to speak those affirmations to yourself every day.

Now, it's your turn. Read through the statements below and identify which stories you believe about yourself. Take note of the old story and receive the truth offered in each line. Create an affirmation that allows you to speak truth to those old stories. Your affirmations should be concise, written in present tense, and represent a clear declaration. Bonus points if you can connect your affirmation to a scripture verse.

Story – I must perform to be accepted.
Truth – You were accepted before you accomplished one thing. You belong here.

Story – I need to prove my worth.
Truth – Your worth is not attached to doing. You are worthy because you exist.

Story – Everything I do must be perfect.
Truth – You are human, not a machine. You deserve the same grace you give to others.

Story – I need to give my all without expecting anything in return.
Truth – Without reciprocity, you will be left with nothing more to give.

Story – It's all on me. I always carry the total burden on my shoulders.
Truth – You were created to depend on your Heavenly Father and live in community. If the burden is heavy, you are shouldering something He did not give you.

Story – I'm behind on my destiny. Everyone else is moving ahead of me.

Truth – There is no competition when you operate in brilliance. The purpose journey is you versus you, and you are the fan favorite.

Story – I am always in competition. I can't let up.

Truth – There's enough room for all of us to heal and thrive. No need to compete.

Story – People are not trustworthy, so I'd rather be alone.

Truth – You were not created to do life alone. God will provide the right people who have the capacity to hold space for you.

Story – Everyone is judging me.

Truth – Most people are consumed by their own lives. They aren't paying attention to you at all. Those who judge are not your concern. God will handle that part. He will also increase your capacity to receive a challenge with love and grace.

Story – I owe everyone who gave me a chance. I have to show them I was a good choice.

Truth – Nothing was given to you for free. You have fought hard for everything you enjoy.

Story – I must play small to make sure I don't make everyone around me uncomfortable.

Truth – Dimming your light does no one any good. You were created to shine, and that's exactly what people need from you.

Story – I dominate in everything I do.
Truth – Accept the grace to learn and grow. There will be messy moments as well as triumphs, and we embrace them all.

Story – I'm used to just surviving, always holding on by a thread.
Truth – You were created to thrive. Just surviving is no longer sufficient.

Story – I hold myself to a higher standard.
Truth – Overperformance is a trap. Unrealistic expectations are not a badge of honor.

Story – I just don't want to miss anything.
Truth – When you live in alignment with your God-given brilliance, what is meant for you cannot miss you.

Story – I'm just waiting my turn. One day, I'll have a seat at the table.
Truth – God promised to prepare a table before you in the presence of your enemies (Psalm 23:5). You don't have to wait to be tapped on the shoulder to walk in purpose.

 Download the *Disrupting Burnout* journal for a fillable copy of this activity at patricebuckner jackson.com/journal or scan the QR code for access.

Chapter 8

Build Your Boundaries

The year 2012 was my year. I'm telling you, the heavens opened and everything I desired at that point poured into my life. In the preceding years, I'd felt like I was drowning in a waiting place. You know that place where you're doing everything you know to do, but it seems nothing you desire comes your way. I was single, childless, and frustrated. I was going the extra mile at work and taking all the extra assignments. I was doing all the things we've been taught a good woman should do. Despite all that, I was just waiting. I was grinding, working, and serving, but none of that effort seemed fruitful. Was there something wrong with me? Was God angry with me? I just didn't understand why it was taking so long. I wondered if I had done something wrong to make me ineligible for the blessings I desired.

Then came 2012. That year, I met, got engaged to, and married the love of my life. Oh yeah, we don't waste time around here! By marrying Edward, I became Mama Patrice to BabyGirl. I completed my coursework towards my doctoral degree; the only thing left to do was write my dissertation. I was also promoted to dean of students at work. As you can see, it was all about me in 2012. I received everything I desired in my life in a matter of months. I was no longer walking on the ground; I was floating through life. It was my year. Until it wasn't.

By October 2012, I was in tears much of the time. Overwhelmed, I didn't know how to carry all my blessings. I quickly realized everything I had longed for, prayed for, and waited for came with new responsibilities. And what was I to do? Was I to go to my new husband, for whom I had waited all my life, and explain that if he'd just show me some grace, I could grind it out at my new job and come back later to be a good wife? Or was I to explain to my new daughter how I was so grateful she wanted me to be a part of her life, but I had school and work going on, and if she would just give me a little grace, then I could come back and build a relationship? Or was I to go to my new boss and explain that I had this wonderful new family and if she would just let me get away with the bare minimum for a little while, I would come back later and do everything I could to do a good job?

None of that was an option. What was I willing to let fall? What was I willing to give up? None of it. I had to find a way to make it all work.

I didn't know how to handle competing priorities without hurting myself and the ones I love. I tried time-management tactics, which allowed me to be more productive at times, but none of them protected me or my family from the consequences of burnout. After all that waiting to have a family, I almost lost them. I tried to make it work for years. The day I left my job in 2019, I was hanging on by a thread because I had no limits. I felt like I had no protection that day when it all fell apart. I needed help. I needed to call somebody to come get me, but I couldn't even open my office door. I was worried because I knew somebody would be standing on the other side of that door who needed me. I was empty and broken.

Failure to set and enforce boundaries in my life left me vulnerable to the Cycle of Burnout. To disrupt that cycle and protect everything and everyone who means most to you, you must build boundaries that protect your soul. Building boundaries is the second HeartWork strategy we need to discuss.

Boundaries Are Safety

Think of your boundaries as the walls of an ancient city. Ancient cities were fortified by a stone wall several feet high and several feet deep. The wall surrounded a city, not for isolation, but for protection. Watchmen on the wall controlled access to the city. They had the authority to let down the drawbridge to allow allies to enter or to welcome citizens back home. The watchmen also had authority to protect the wall from a breach of any kind. You are responsible for watching over your boundaries as they watched over those city walls. You determine who or what may gain access to your soul.

If you do not have boundary walls, your soul is vulnerable, exposed, and trapped in the Cycle of Burnout. If you do not honor your walls, you might as well not have them. When your walls are weak, you lose control over access to your soul. When you fail to honor your walls, you allow everything and every person to have access to you.

Here are some signs you need more or stronger boundaries:

- You find yourself resentful in helping others.

- You say yes, but you become frustrated when you need to carry out the yes.
- You have trouble saying no.
- You have a strong desire to isolate yourself so no one else asks you for anything.
- You fail to connect with others because you're afraid they will need something from you.
- Working, serving, and giving are in conflict in your heart.
- You feel responsible for rescuing others.
- You feel misused or abused.
- People take advantage of your kindness.
- You often think, "What will they do without me?"

Adopting someone else's boundary that catches your attention on social media is not enough. My friend, Dr. Raymona Lawrence, calls this boundary borrowing "imposter boundaries." Imposter boundaries will be more of a hindrance than help to you because the boundaries of another person will not be a fit for your needs. Just observing a list of rules for your life isn't the answer here. Boundaries go beyond a cute social media post or a scribble in your new journal. Boundaries that work must be based on your values, the precious aspects of your life that you are unwilling to lose. Boundaries protect what means most to you.

Boundaries Give You Control

It's a mistake to think your boundaries will control any other person. Your boundaries should focus on your own behavior. Psychologist, professor, and host of the *Mind Your Mental* podcast, Dr. Raquel Martin, offers an example of a boundary on her Instagram post called "Boundaries vs. Rules." "When you raise your voice, I will not engage." This boundary allows the other person to raise their voice if they desire, but the woman with boundaries has decided how she will (or will not) respond. Boundary work is very specific. You need to make sure your energy is being spent in the most productive ways. When I say energy, I'm referring to your time, effort, emotions, and attention. You have a limited supply of energy, so you must be a good steward of it. You cannot fix all the things, and some things are not yours to fix.

To be effective in building boundaries, you need to establish your line of ownership. I call this your "no" line. Think of the no line like a property line for your soul. To build a fence in your yard, you must first identify where your neighbor's property ends and yours begins. Where is the property line for what physically, mentally, and spiritually belongs to you? Where is the line between the action you need to take and the work that belongs to another person in your life? Building boundaries is about controlling what you need to control and releasing what does not belong to you.

As I coach my clients, I find many women cannot differentiate between their own responsibilities and the responsibilities of others. They submerge themselves in the ideas, opinions, and traumas of others so often that they cannot tell the difference between their baggage and the baggage of another person. Their compassion drives them to dive deeply into other people's worlds. The danger of that compassionate drive when they haven't identified their no line is they take personal responsibility for someone else's journey.

Whose baggage are you carrying? Does it belong to your spouse, child, parents, coworker, or boss? Whose bags have you picked up because you failed to realize you'd crossed your own no line? You must learn how to set boundaries that allow you to serve to the level you're called to serve while giving your people the honor of their own journey, choices, and decisions. If not, your help turns into a hindrance for the people you care so much about, and you become a stumbling block for the people you desire to help.

In *The Critically Reflective Practitioner*,[1] Sue and Neil Thompson present the CIA framework, which stands for control, influence, and accept, as a guideline for working through challenges of leadership. Many practitioners use this model as a tool for stress management, but it's also exceptionally powerful in helping you build your boundaries. Allow me to add a little spoonful of PBJ to the CIA model. Let's walk through it to determine how you can make the best use of your energy.

Let's start with the most difficult part first, accept. If you are a fixer, this phase will be challenging. Here, you begin to release things that are not in your control. Specifically, if you don't have knowledge, skills, ability, experience, access, *and* authority to make progress in a specific area, you need to release it. This is the no line. Accepting doesn't mean you don't care. Nor does acceptance mean you're not directly impacted. Acceptance means you realize you are not in a position to make change or progress in that area, so you decide to stop putting energy there.

During the pandemic of 2020, I could not control political decisions or COVID mandates. I was directly impacted by many decisions concerning my job, but I had no access or authority to do anything about them. I had to redirect my time, attention, emotions, and efforts to areas where I could make some progress, like protecting my own health, caring for my family, and responding to the needs of my students. I found there was plenty I could accomplish within my own control without wasting energy in areas I could not control. Continuing to toil in areas where you need to accept will make you feel like a hamster on a wheel, exhausted and making no progress. A lack of progress fuels frustration, and lingering frustration is a portal directly into the Cycle of Burnout.

Here's the tricky part about acceptance. You may very well have knowledge, skills, ability, and experience in the area. You may even have the right answer, but Friend, if you don't have access and authority, you're not in a position to make progress there. Accepting does not mean you will never give energy in this area. It just means, at the current moment, accepting is the most productive thing for you to do. You can revisit and make a different decision if circumstances change in the future.

Consider all the challenges taking up mental real estate in your heart right now: challenges at work, family members you're concerned for, the state of the world. Are you equipped and positioned to make a difference in these areas? If so, make a plan and take action. If not, you need to release it. Release it in prayer. Release it through journaling. Do whatever you need to do to let that go so you can make the most productive use of your energy.

Now let's move on to influence. You need to put *some* energy where you have influence, but not most of your energy. Influence means you have access. You may have the ear of the decision-maker, or a seat at the table, or some other way to make a positive impact, but complete authority does not belong to you. With influence, either the full decision is up to someone else or you need to collaborate to make the decision. In your areas of influence, you have some knowledge, skills, ability, experience, and access, but the authority lies with another person or involves another person.

My BabyGirl is in her early twenties, and I accept I do not control her life. Honestly, I didn't control her when she was twelve. The authority was always her own. Edward and I have major influence in her life through the ways we love her, support her, teach her, and model for her, but the decisions about her life are hers. We're fortunate that her decisions often align with our family values, but we don't take credit for that just like we don't take responsibility when her decisions fail to align with our values. The authority, decisions, and consequences all belong to BabyGirl. I honor my influence in her life and intentionally decide how I need to apply that influence, but I always respect her authority to decide.

Where do you have influence and how do you want to use it? Who else is involved or impacted? Who has authority in each area? What access to or influence on the people involved do you have? How do you want to use that influence?

Let's look at some influential actions to consider.

Say something. Share your thoughts, opinions, concerns, and ideas. Be empowered to share even when your opinion deviates from the majority's thoughts on the matter. Determine when you feel safe enough to speak up. Your voice matters, and you have something to say.

Show up. Do not underestimate the power of your presence. Sometimes just being in the room has an impact. Show up at school events for your children. Be seen at extra work events. Show up at the town hall meeting. Be present even when you have nothing to say. Your presence brings influence.

Choose silence. Sometimes the most powerful thing we can do is be silent. Our culture is uncomfortable with silence. We feel pressure to fill the air with knowledge and solutions. However, there are times when our solutions are not helpful. It's amazing how people can figure things out when we don't automatically swoop in to save the day. Make space for folks to use their own minds. Allow your silence to provoke your people to problem-solve for themselves.

Now, let's talk about control. If you have knowledge, skills, ability, experience, access, *and* authority, you have control, Friend. These are the areas in your life where you will see the most progress. These are the areas where you should invest your time, attention, efforts, and emotion. The ball is in your court. What is in your control?

Concerning my health, I don't control my DNA, but I do control how I move my body and what I eat. Concerning my family, I don't control the actions of my husband or my daughter, but I control how I love them and how I share my own needs and boundaries with them. Concerning my faith, I don't control God. I cannot manipulate Him to do what I want Him to do, but I do control my own spiritual disciplines. I have full authority on how I express my faith and how I grow in faith through my dedication to disciplines like prayer, reading, worship, and giving.

By focusing on what you control, you will see the most progress in the areas that mean most to you. What do you control, Friend? What actions have you identified that are completely within your authority? Your boundaries are about your own control.

Build Your Boundaries

Building boundaries that work starts with determining your values. This is not about philosophical ideas of integrity. Instead, consider the aspects of life that mean the most to you. Simply put, what are you unwilling to lose? Remember burnout is a thief. It comes to steal everything that means most to you. When I was burned out, my health, my most significant relationships, and my faith were all in jeopardy. I didn't take care of my body. My child felt like she needed an appointment to spend time with me while I was available for everyone else's children, and my spiritual disciplines were all lacking. I was a mess. I left everything that meant the most to me vulnerable in the name of doing good for others. I had no walls.

Look around you. Is there anything significant to you that's damaged right now? Are your body, mind, heart, or relationships screaming out to you for change? What means most to you in the whole wide world? If you were forced to give it all up, what would hurt you most to release?

I am unwilling to lose . . .

- My time
- My family
- My health
- My faith

Your turn. What are you unwilling to lose? Write your list in your *Disrupting Burnout* journal.

The next step of building boundaries is to establish your anchor. Your why is your anchor because the power is always in the why.

Why are you unwilling to lose those pieces of your life? It's one thing to declare your health is important to you, but it doesn't become personal until you know why. Without the why, you may resort to what culture or other people have determined should be most important to you instead of what matters to your own soul.

After you make a list of what you are unwilling to lose, write *why* that part of your life is so important to you. Document your anchor for each core value. Why are you unwilling to lose each valued element of your life? Make sure the why is your own and not what you feel you need to say.

Let's look at my value of time for example:

> Time is the only resource I cannot make, buy, or find more of. We all have the same limited amount of time as long as we wake up and breathe. It is my responsibility to maximize this valuable resource freely given to me by God.

Your turn. Why is each value so precious to you? Write your why for each value in your *Disrupting Burnout* journal.

Now that you've established your values and you know why each is important to you, imagine a new normal in each area. What do you want to see? What do you want to experience? What do you want your life to look like? Be specific, Friend. Write the vision and release the outcome. Write exactly what you would love to see with no pressure to produce exactly what you wrote.

Don't limit your vision to just what you believe you can produce. This is an opportunity to "give God something to bless," as my coach Patrice Washington encourages us to do. Make room for His super to be added to your natural. Dream, Friend! Write the vision for each value.

Here is an example of my vision for my time:

> I envision productive days with extra time to do nothing
> whenever I desire. I only want to work Monday to Thursday,
> 10am to 4pm, unless I am on a work trip. I desire time to
> explore the cities as I travel and not just work time. I want
> evenings and weekends free for family time and quarterly
> alone time just for PBJ. Each month, I want to take some
> time away for prayer, rest, and thinking. I desire more time
> with friends and family through phone calls and in person.
> These calls will be to catch up, laugh, and encourage each
> other—not to resolve crises. I will visit my mama at least
> once per quarter and spend quality time with my nieces
> and nephews.

What is your vision for each value listed? Write it as you want
to see it.

Next, you need to establish your no line. Refer to the CIA model
and determine what you control, where you have influence, and
what you need to accept concerning each value.

Accept, Influence, Control

- I control the time I wake up.
- I influence how we spend family time in the evenings and
  on weekends.
- I control my work schedule on days I'm not speaking or train-
  ing. I have influence on my speaking and training schedule.
- I control the number of appointments I take each week.
- I control the amount of time I preserve between meetings.

- I accept that sometimes projects take longer than I expected.
- I accept that I cannot control how others feel about my time boundaries.

What do you accept, influence, and control with respect to each value?

Finally, it's time to decide what you're willing to do to protect your values. Friend, this is where you begin to draw a line in the sand. What needs to change? What action can you take to preserve the values in your life? This doesn't always have to be a complete overhaul. It's amazing how small, simple, seemingly insignificant steps can transform your life.

Before you jump into action, let's have a little chat about effective action. Nothing derails belief faster than attempting gigantic change and failing. Often, when achievers think about action, your mind immediately goes to big leaps. You want to conquer, to win, and to be the best. You also want to minimize discomfort and the time it takes to complete the task as much as possible. You look at a big goal and attempt to accomplish it in the smallest possible amount of time, which often leads to abandoning the goal. The truth is big goals are only accomplished one small step at a time.

In my podcast interview with Lia Valencia Key, who I'll share more about in chapter 9, Lia describes what she calls "one-millimeter movement."[2] As a jewelry designer, one millimeter is the smallest measurement on her ruler, but it makes a tremendous difference in the outcome of a piece of jewelry. One millimeter seems so insignificant when most of us look at the project, but Lia explains how it's possible to have two extraordinarily different products by adding or subtracting just one millimeter. She encourages people to consider the power of one-millimeter movement toward your goals. What is one small change you could make today that could have a powerful impact months from now?

My friend Morgan Davis shared a similar thought while speaking to a group of college students about physical wellness. Morgan is a coordinator of a wellness program at a university and a personal trainer. At this college event, a student asked Morgan her thoughts on how to stay consistent when creating healthy habits. Morgan shared that fitness professionals often encourage their clients to be one percent better each day. Just one percent. If you know you need to drink more water, don't start by tackling a whole gallon. Add one more bottle each day this week or twenty more ounces than yesterday. Instead of going from junk food to vegan, maybe consider adding more greens as a side to your pizza or have one more serving of fruits and vegetables each day. Instead of going from sedentary to running a marathon, consider adding thirty minutes of movement you enjoy to each day.

Morgan shared how as your body experiences the benefits of incorporating small healthy actions, you'll begin to crave them, and as a result, those new healthy actions will eventually become habits. Instead of shocking your body with a tremendous, unsustainable change, consider how you might be one percent better than yesterday. Allow small actions to create a consistency that brings transformation.

Friend, I know honoring small steps is unpopular. In Western society, we like fast food, microwave meals, and quick change, but it's important to know the human body does not respond well to quick, tremendous change. Gabi Ruth, creator and host of the *Pain to Passion Live* podcast, encourages us to work with our bodies to accomplish our goals instead of working against them. Gabi teaches her community how the body naturally responds to change and how to show compassion for your normal functions in order to stretch out of a comfort zone.

According to Gabi, your vagus nerve scans your environment for danger and alerts the brain when danger is detected. Change is processed as danger in your brain. As a result, the brain activates your fight, flight, or freeze responses without your knowledge or permission. When the vagus nerve senses danger, your brain reacts in the same way it would if you were being chased by a lion. This is a natural, automatic process that occurs in a healthy body. This is what your nervous system was created to do. Learning to work with this process places you in position to succeed with your goals without being halted by your natural responses to threat.

In an interview on the *Disrupting Burnout* podcast, on an episode called "Show Yourself Compassion," Gabi shares that to stretch yourself into new habits, you need to keep one foot in your comfort zone and one foot slightly outside of your comfort zone. [3] She explains that when you keep one foot in your comfort zone, stretch one foot out of that comfortable area, and use regulating actions to remind your brain that you're safe, you begin to stretch your comfort zone into new areas. As you become comfortable with the new spot, you may decide to step out again to make that comfort zone even wider.

Remember this action should be taken step by step, pausing at each step to allow your brain time to adjust and acclimate to the new action or environment. Practice self-compassion by understanding the natural processes of your body and working in collaboration with those processes to experience lasting transformation. Make one-millimeter movements. Be one percent better.

Now is the time for action. What are you willing to do to protect your values? The goal of this question is not to force you into any specific action. The goal here is for you to declare the action you're willing to take to establish your boundaries. Change doesn't happen without action.

In this step, you'll choose an action that will lead to your new vision. Friend, do not get stuck here. Make a choice. There's always an opportunity to revisit and revise. This is not about perfection; we're looking for progress.

Here's an example based on my value of time:

- I will prioritize time with God by waking up at 5 am each weekday morning.
- I will create time just to think, vision, and problem-solve by setting weekly "Think" appointments on my calendar. These appointments will be at least one hour, three days per week.
- I will not accept unscheduled business calls. I am no longer on call. All business communication must be scheduled at least two days in advance.
- I will keep my phone on "Do Not Disturb" during work hours, devotion time, and family time to preserve my focus and energy.

Grab your *Disrupting Burnout* journal and write the actions you're willing to take to protect each of your values. These are your boundaries.

Do the Heart Work

Let's practice using the CIA method for a different purpose. Do you ever find yourself with more to-do list than time? How do you identify the priorities of the priorities? This activity allows you to practice an alternative use of the method.

Complete an energy audit.

This audit should be focused on the tasks, decisions, and ideas cluttering your mind right now. The focus of the energy audit is to assist you in choosing priorities when everything seems urgent and important. How do you intentionally decide where to invest your time, effort, attention, and emotions? Take the following steps to declutter your to-do list.

1. List five people, problems, concerns, decisions, or responsibilities taking up space in your mind right now.
2. In which areas are you lacking access and authority? Review the list to determine what you need to accept.
3. Where do you have influence, and how do you want to use your influence to make a positive impact?
4. Where do you have control, and what do you want to do about it?

135

 Download the *Disrupting Burnout* journal for a fillable copy of this activity at patricebuckner jackson.com/journal or scan the QR code for access.

Chapter 9

Boundaries That Work

When I think about boundaries that work, I think about my client Lexi. I met Lexi, a statuesque, chocolate-skinned woman with a magnetic smile, at a conference where I served as the keynote speaker. I noticed her as soon as she entered the room, and so did many other people. I marveled as colleagues from all over her state flocked to greet her. During my speech, I noticed her locked in on every word, and I felt her Spirit drawing the best out of me. After my speech, Lexi came over to greet me and thank me for my speech. I felt compelled to share with her the brilliance I saw in her, and we shared a precious moment right there in the ballroom.

Lexi followed up a few weeks later and became my first one-on-one client. She explained to me how she'd hit a ceiling at her institution, with no upward mobility in sight, and as her 40th birthday approached, she felt pressed to do what she was created to do. However, she wasn't sure what that was or how to do it. Lexi had checked all the boxes. She was a good daughter and sister and a phenomenal auntie. She was completing her PhD and had garnered respect in her field and in her state. She was active with her sorority and dedicated to community service. She had done all the things we learn success is made of but still felt like something was missing.

Through the HeartWork strategies, we explored Lexi's path from childhood to the time of our meeting, identifying evidence of her brilliance along the way. Lexi created new boundaries to support the life she desired to live by excluding the opinions and limitations of others from her decision-making, releasing relationships that no longer served her, and taking bold steps toward the life she desired. Lexi decided to live where she wanted to live and pursue professional goals that may or may not be supported by her colleagues. With every new, unapologetic step, she gained new freedom.

When we first met, Lexi had a strong desire to keep our work together private, a preference I often see with educators. People who may consider doing something different with their life often have a fear of judgment or repercussions. With Lexi, that fear didn't last. Before I knew it, she was shining her brilliance all over social media! She also walked away from a long-term relationship, moved into a new home, and regained her joy. Lexi is now aligning her professional goals with the personal dreams of her heart and becoming a sought-after transformational speaker. She's creating the life she desires.

Remember boundaries that work must be connected to your personal values. Boundaries are often discussed as what we won't do or won't allow in our lives. However, effective boundaries are not limited to what we need to disallow. Your boundaries must protect what means most to you. Sometimes that means adding new action or perspectives to your life. As the watchman on your boundary wall, you may restrict, or you may allow. You have authority to remove, and you have authority to add. Do not limit the action necessary to protect your values. As you consider what new boundaries you need to apply, I want to share some practical boundaries for you to consider. As you read these life lessons, consider the places in your life where you may need a bit more protection.

Watch Your Mouth

You will have exactly what you say. The most powerful catalyst to your transformation is your own words. As you learned in chapter 7 when we discussed creating belief, you are living today in the results of words you spoke yesterday. Romans 4:17 teaches us we serve a God who creates something out of nothing through His words. Just like in the beginning when He said, "Let there be," and it was, we are admonished to speak our freedom and brilliance into existence (Genesis 1:3-25).

Learning to make confessions in alignment with your purpose is the key to your brilliant future. According to Proverbs 18:21, "The tongue can bring death or life; those who love to talk will reap the consequences." Your words create your belief systems because God created our brains to change as we speak.

Kobe Campbell, trauma therapist and author of *Why Am I Like This*,[1] explains how the brain is equipped with neuroplasticity, which allows it to change as our beliefs change. Our belief systems are built on neural pathways, which are like highways in the brain. As we speak, we create new belief highways. You will have what you say. Kobe explains it this way: "We will believe most intensely what we hear most often." Your words have the power to create your future. Use your words to manifest the brilliance God created you to express.

In my podcast interview with Lia Valencia Key,[2] founder and creative force behind Valencia Key jewelry, Lia shares how her dream to become the global hair and makeup stylist for the shopping network QVC came to be her reality. She endured several rejections as she pursued the position. She worked odd jobs, like sweeping a salon floor, selling department store cosmetics, and bartending in preparation for the dream to come true. Lia did everything she could control. She completed cosmetology school, got licensed, swept that salon floor so she could learn how to do all types of hair, and practiced her make-up application skills by selling a national brand in a department store. However, the most powerful thing she did to manifest this dream was to speak it often to everyone.

Lia told everyone who would listen that she would one day be the global hair and makeup stylist for QVC. She made this declaration for five or six years until, one night, she said it to a customer as she served his drink. She had no idea who the guy was when she said it, but this person connected her to the right people at QVC, and those people opened the door for her to audition for the position—and the rest is history! Through the power of confession Lia created belief in herself and in the people she spoke the dream to. She was so convinced, after several years of confessing the dream, that she convinced this stranger to support her and become a reference for her. Friend, the power of change is in believing, and you will birth belief through confession. You need to say it.

Base your confessions in what God says about you. Only say what He says. Trust God more than you trust yourself. Trust Him first. There is a dangerous movement in culture right now that places self above all. Our culture is becoming self-righteous in the name of self-care. Be careful, Friend.

Jeremiah 17:5-10

> This is what the LORD says: "Cursed are those who put their trust in mere humans who rely on human strength and turn their hearts away from the LORD. They are like stunted shrubs in the desert, with no hope for the future. They will live in the barren wilderness, in an uninhabited salty land.

> "But blessed are those who trust in the LORD and have made the LORD their hope and confidence. They are like trees planted along a riverbank, with roots that reach deep into the water. Such trees are not bothered by the heat or worried by long months of drought. Their leaves stay green, and they never stop producing fruit.

> "The human heart is the most deceitful of all things, and desperately wicked. Who really knows how bad it is? But I, the LORD, search all hearts and examine secret motives. I give all people their due rewards, according to what their actions deserve."

Your plan is unreliable because you cannot see every step in the process. Why wouldn't you believe in the One who created you before you trusted in yourself? The Bible never said you should believe in yourself; culture teaches that lesson. As a woman of God, you are called to trust and rely wholly on Him.

Trusting God above yourself is not about self-deprecation; it's about keeping things in proper order. Trusting God first means trusting who He made you to be and trusting the gifts He instilled in you. Refusing to make decisions based on your emotions doesn't mean you have low self-esteem, lack of confidence, or any inaccurate view of yourself. Trusting God first means you know everything you need is in Him, not up to you, and you make decisions accordingly. There is no fullness of purpose without the God who created you for the purpose. As a daughter of the King, you do not have to strive, fight, or beg. Everything you need is in Him. Trusting God first means your belief and confidence rest in the flawless God who made you flawlessly. It means the same God who created the heavens and earth made you. The same God who makes no mistakes formed you with His own hands. If God is perfect (and He is), how would He make a mistake with you? You mean to tell me He perfectly made heaven and earth but made a mistake with you? I don't think so, Friend.

Relying on our perfect God does not mean your life will be perfect. Perfection isn't possible while we live on this earth where human beings have free will. However, it does mean a perfect God will cause all imperfections to work in your favor, perfectly. When you trust God above yourself, the weight of your destiny is not on you, but on Him. You don't have to live in anxiety, worrying about messing things up. When you trust Him and confess His Word, His plans manifest in your life.

Don't be out here confessing anything that wasn't meant for you. You may get it, but you won't be able to handle it. When you trust God and speak His Word, the outcome is on Him. Your future is secure because you trust God first and repeat what He has already said about you in His Word. Base your confession on the Word of God and watch His plan for you unfold.

If you struggle with speaking life to yourself, practice speaking positively while looking at yourself in a mirror. If a mirror feels too awkward, grab a picture of your younger self and speak lovingly to her. Thank her for getting you so far and affirm her future to her. You need practice speaking to yourself in the powerful way you speak to others. Give it a try. You will see the growth and beauty positive words can bring.

Guard Your Heart

As boundaries are for your protection, we need to discuss how you must guard your heart. In Proverbs 4:23, King Solomon, considered one of the wisest men to ever live, encouraged us: "Guard your heart above all else, for it determines the course of your life." In this scripture, the word heart refers to your soul- the mind, will, and emotions.[3] King Solomon's words teach us how what we think impacts every area of our lives.

Begin with what you think. Set guards around your thoughts. You cannot control every thought that pops into your head, but you can control how long you meditate on the thought. You can decide that negative thoughts will be immediately tossed aside and you will spend your time meditating on positive thoughts about yourself and about the world around you.

Consider what you feed your mind. Garbage in, garbage out. Power in, power out. This is why studying the Bible is so important. The Word of God is alive, and it transforms your thoughts as you consume it. Anything you meditate on will transform your thoughts. Choose media, conversations, and self-talk that edifies your mind and Spirit. Reject any music, media, conversations, or entertainment that does not align with your God-given brilliance. Refuse to entertain any thought that does not bring life. It's counterproductive to do this HeartWork and then entertain input that exalts an opposing idea. Guard your heart by making intentional positive choices concerning your thoughts.

Accept Help

In March 2020, when we were sent home to work, it was quite an adjustment for my family. I worked from a makeup table in our bedroom while my husband worked from the office in our home. Our daughter was sent home from college to study online, and our dog was wondering why we were all in her space. I attended Zoom meetings from early morning until late in the evening, trying to figure out how to do our work differently than we had ever done it, while my family often finished their day earlier than I did.

Prior to the pandemic, the tradition in our family was that I cooked. I enjoy cooking, and my family enjoys the meals. We all expected this tradition to continue to work—until it did not. One evening, after I had worked until about eight o'clock, I emerged from the bedroom to find my loving family sitting on the couch, chatting, laughing, and watching a movie. I asked, "Did y'all eat?" "We were waiting on you," they replied.

Their answer was like an atomic bomb in my head. I lost it. I don't remember what I said, but there were tears, mostly mine. I was so frustrated that they hadn't taken the initiative to handle dinner when they knew my current workload. I felt unloved and unappreciated. They felt confused.

The truth is I'm not easy to help. My family didn't think I wanted them to help me. I did all the household tasks while holding a full-time job. It wore me out and made me frustrated, but I never said anything. I got angrier and angrier over time, but I just allowed it to fester. My family had no idea until it came boiling out of me that day. I just couldn't hold it anymore. The extra stress from work and a global pandemic broke the levees of my emotions.

After I let it all out, my family explained they had no idea I desired their help. They assumed I preferred to do it myself, and for good reason. I made them believe I preferred to do it myself. Anytime they helped, I critiqued, tried to manage every step, or just took over. The truth was I wanted help. I needed help, but my controlling nature blocked me from the help I so desperately needed. That day, I decided I wanted rest more than I wanted to be right all the time.

Together, we created a new standard. They agreed to jump in on housework and to take care of dinner if I hadn't finished working by 5:30 pm. I agreed to just say thank you. No matter what dinner they chose or whether the chore was done to my standard, I was willing to be grateful. That boundary helped us through our tele-working experience and encouraged me to establish boundaries in other areas of my life.

So I created a boundary that I'm willing to accept help. I am a proud, strong, independent woman. (Some may call me stubborn, but let's just agree on independent.) Helpers don't always receive help well. You may prefer to suffer through a situation before making your need for help known. The truth is all of us could use a little help every now and then. Accepting help does not make you weak or needy. It means you are wise enough to know your limits. It means you have chosen peace over pride.

I must admit I struggled to accept help due to stories I still carried from childhood. As a young child, I watched my family members clean houses for work. A couple of times when I couldn't go to school, my favorite aunt took me with her to clean the house of a prominent woman in our town. Although the family was kind to and appreciative of my aunt, something in me didn't like that she had to do this work. I could not imagine having the responsibilities of cleaning my own house and someone else's house too. At five or six years old, it didn't seem fair to me that my aunt had to clean the houses of able-bodied folks. I grew up in a very small community with traditional values that dictated a good woman take care of her own home. What kind of lazy woman couldn't even clean her own house? That's what I thought back then before I had my own house and many responsibilities.

Auntie eventually completed her degree and moved on to do the work of her heart in early childhood education, but those experiences stuck with me. I worked my tail off in school to give myself career choices. I was determined to do what I wanted to do instead of what I had to do. When my life got so full that things were falling off my plate, I couldn't bring myself to hire help for my home. My story was I didn't want to treat those folks like people treated my aunt. Now, remember I said the people Auntie worked for were very kind, but in my young mind, they were lazy and unfair to her. Since I didn't want to be lazy or unfair, when I needed help, I did not seek it. I didn't want to put my responsibilities on another person.

I didn't release this story until I heard a professional woman I admire speaking about seeking support. She described how the woman who assisted her in her home ran a small business, giving jobs to women who could make their own hours. My mind shifted; instead of being unfair, maybe accepting help could be empowering to another person. I could support a woman-owned small business while getting the relief I so desperately needed.

I interviewed several women and chose the person I felt was the best fit for our home. I learned I didn't have to do it all myself to be a "good woman." Just because it's my responsibility that doesn't mean I personally have to do it. Accepting help has freed me to pursue brilliance and allowed me to bless so many people who have supported me along the way.

You can find help in technology, services, and the people around you. I invest in technology ranging from robot vacuum cleaners to wi-fi enabled crockpots. I utilize a variety of services, including housecleaning, meal prep, and grocery delivery. I also invite family, friends, and experts to support me in my ministry, business, and personal life. In many cases, I could do it myself, but why should I? Old mindsets, like "A good woman keeps her own home," come up every now and then, but I've learned to silence that voice. Inviting help has freed my time and attention and allowed me to accomplish things only I can do, like writing this book and spending quality time with my husband.

Consider how much time you could reclaim if you invited help into your life. Do not allow money to be a barrier. Some of these services cost money, and you should invest if you can, but if you don't have the means right now, there are still people in your life who want to help you. You will be amazed how help will find you if you just state your need. Tell a friend. Share with a small group at church. If you're willing to state the need, God is loving enough to send the support. Ask for help, Friend.

Can we talk about delegating at work for a minute? As I was promoted through leadership, I found I had a hard time delegating to my team. It seemed easier just to do it myself, and I never wanted to put too much pressure on my staff. I wanted to carry all the pressure while taking care of them. Well, we all know how that approach turned out.

Do you remember the kid in school who did the whole group project alone because they didn't trust their group mates to get it done? Are you that kid? Do you find yourself doing the same thing at work today? It's just easier to do it all yourself, until it all becomes too much.

That "I can do it myself" mentality was cool before you got married, had children, or were promoted to lead several teams, several departments, and several projects. At this level, trying to do it all yourself is detrimental. You may be holding up the progress of the entire team because you're trying to do it alone. Consider this. People want to help. They want to grow. Many colleagues are honored when you trust them enough to give them a major task. The boundary of delegation is one I have truly honed in my professional life. It's time to learn to delegate. Yes, I said "learn" because this may not come naturally to you.

Delegation is an investment. Just like a financial investment, it may not immediately pay large dividends. Delegation requires dedicating time and energy on the front end to teach people your standard. Invest in the person and the work enough to give them the information and the tools they need to succeed. If you do this well, it will pay off tremendously in due time. Investing in your people first garners loyalty, not just to the organization, but also to you, the leader. We're not talking manipulation here. Invest in a genuine way that says, "You matter to me, and I want the best for you."

When you delegate, make sure you communicate your needs and expectations clearly. You are so good at carrying your heavy load that you make it all look too easy. You look like you have it all together, but the truth is you could really use some help. You really need someone to take something off your plate. You may be frustrated that people around you don't offer help, but, Friend, you don't look like you need help. You're so focused on making it all work that you don't leave room for anyone to support you. I encourage you to say it. Say it to the people in your household. Say it to the people you work with. Be specific about how people can help you, but also leave some room for them to do it their way. No micromanaging. No expectation of perfection. Just accept the help. Every now and then, consider relaxing the standard and allow peace to be the priority of the moment.

There are people in your life who love you enough to help you. Others want to learn from you enough to take something off your plate. Make room for others to help you. State your needs and accept the help.

The Power of No

This one goes out to all my people pleasers. You are my people. I get you. You're a nurturer. Lots of people depend on you. You feel purpose in taking care of others—that is, until you've taken on too much. At that point, you need a rock to hide behind because you hate going back on your word. You may prefer to try to do it all, at whatever expense, instead of saying no.

My need to please has cost me several relationships in my life. I've led people to believe I would always be there, wherever and whenever they needed me. When I made the promise, I really meant it. However, I often failed to count the cost of every yes. Before I knew it, I had overcommitted again. This challenge finally caused me to analyze my role in relationships. I love hard, and I take care of people. I am a nurturer, and I am good at it. I make people feel cared for and safe, but I had to come to terms with the fact that my nurturing nature may be more about me than I like to admit. As I shared in chapter 7, my heart believes all these people need me, but the truth of the matter is I have a need to be needed. It caused me to create expectations that ultimately, I was unable to fulfill, often leading to a broken relationship. My natural response is to hide in shame in those situations, but I'm training myself to prevent this scenario by being extremely honest and selective about my commitments.

A few years ago, during a conversation about family responsibilities, my friend Dorsey shared one line I have never forgotten. She said, "Patrice, I am learning to say no so I can have better yeses." That statement struck me like a lightning bolt. Not long after this conversation, Dorsey resigned her position and went home to take care of her babies. Her resignation fueled mixed emotions for me as I was her supervisor at the time, but I could not help but applaud her courage. She had a newborn and two older children who needed her time. Sometimes, we must give up a good yes to enjoy a great yes. We get so caught up with the fear of missing out on what could be that we lose sight of what is right now. I encourage you to learn how to say no to have a better yes.

Since saying no doesn't come easy, I encourage you to implement some safeguards for yourself. These safeguards will protect you from overcommitment and assist you in preserving relationships. Remember you are not obligated to give an immediate answer to a request. Your first answer, without counting the cost, may naturally be yes. Layer in some time to consider your calendar and your other commitments prior to giving an answer. Instead of saying yes, your response might be: "Thanks so much for considering me. What's your deadline for an answer?" This allows you to plan and practice how to say no if no is the answer.

Saying no does not have to be aggressive or traumatic. Consider the following ways of saying no:

- I'm so sorry. I'm not available this time.
- That's not something I do well, but have you considered [insert the name of a person who is talented in the required area]?
- That's just not a good fit for me, but I hope things come together well.
- Please select someone who can give this project the time it deserves. My calendar won't allow it at this time.
- You know that sounds like so much fun, but I won't make it this time.

As a final suggestion, try just saying no. You are not always obligated to give a reason. No is a complete statement on its own. Honesty is love, Friend. People prefer truth even when the answer doesn't align with their preference. Try one of these ways of giving this powerful response and enjoy the rewards of time to do other things.

Another technique I've found effective in helping me say no is strong accountability— and its name is Edward Jackson. My husband is not a person who has trouble saying no. As a matter of fact, Edward has a "no" anointing. While my default is yes, his default is a firm no. There is some real balance there, Friends. My husband is especially sharp at saying no when it comes to commitments of time. Don't get me wrong. He trusts my judgment and will ultimately support whatever I decide in most cases, but he makes his concerns known and helps me see all sides of the situation.

Edward has seen what happens to me when I overcommit. He's familiar with the anxiety and stress that result when I take on too much. He has seen my struggle and stands beside me when I suffer because of overwhelm, so his input matters. He's critical of every request that comes my way. He allows me to be me, but he loves me enough to encourage me to think critically before committing to one more person, project, or invitation. I'm grateful for his accountability.

Sacrifice

We cannot talk about boundaries without talking about sacrifice. Let's go back to 2012. I completed my coursework for my doctorate degree that year, but I didn't graduate until 2016. Yes, Friend, four years later. If you're doing the math, you're correct. It took me seven whole years to complete a four-year doctoral program. The first three years went by easily, but when the blessings of 2012 hit, school was one of the things I allowed to slip. I stopped writing.

I used my family as an excuse. I used my job as an excuse. I was convinced these were very good excuses, and I reached the point where I considered just dropping out of school. We only get a certain number of years to complete the degree, and I had almost reached the deadline.

Everything turned around for me when my lead professor, Dr. Teri Melton, got ahold of me. I had been avoiding her, so she came to my house. This woman came to my door, unannounced, sat at my dining room table, looked me in the eyes, and challenged the thought that I no longer wanted the degree. She got me all the way together. She helped me create an action plan, and she also invited me to speak on a panel for incoming doctoral candidates.

I was confused. *Don't you want the new candidates to be excited about this journey? Don't you need examples of people excelling in the program, not people like me who are bringing the graduation rate down?* I said yes, of course. Any woman who will show up at your house to get your attention is convincing.

After speaking on the panel, I realized she'd asked me to attend for me, not for the audience. I heard so many stories of people who had good excuses to quit. Many people on the panel had several small children at home. One person was recovering from cancer, and another was enduring a dangerous pregnancy. Someone else was caring for elderly parents. When it was my turn, I shared how demanding my job was, but I had to admit in front of the crowd that my biggest hurdle was my own self-sabotage. I had convinced myself I was not a writer and my life was too full to do this right now.

That panel taught me everyone has a story. The difference-maker is what they're willing to do about it. Afterwards, I got my butt in gear, and I graduated one year later. I took on a make-no-excuses attitude and got it done. It took me one year to accomplish something I ran from for three years.

I began to make sacrifices instead of making excuses. I had a meeting with my family where I solicited their prayers, support, and investment. They took on extra chores and gave me grace to spend extensive amounts of time away from them to get this done. I gave up TV and social events for some time and turned my phone off during writing sessions. I dedicated a space in the back of the house as my writing space so I wouldn't be distracted by anything or anyone. I sacrificed sleep on occasion and even took days off from work to get my writing done. I became accountable to my faculty members, and I stopped meditating on negative thoughts. I couldn't afford it. Even in the midst of feeling not enough, I did it anyway. And I got it done.

> *Anything that will serve you well for the rest of your life is worth temporary sacrifice.*

In December 2016, I crossed the stage in front of a roaring crowd as one of my greatest friends, Dr. Raymona Lawrence, proclaimed my new name, "Doctor Patrice Buckner Jackson," and Dr. Teri Melton placed my doctoral hood around my neck. My victory was a victory for many, but it could not have happened without sacrifice.

Choose the Priority of the Moment

Remember our example of carrying all the dumbbell weights in the work-life balance section of chapter 3? Instead of carrying all your weight at the same time, consider how holding one weight at a time might lighten your load. I call this method choosing the priority of the moment. Please note, I specifically said priority "of the moment" because priorities change quickly, and you need to be ready to pivot. As an example, at this current moment, the weight I'm carrying is writing this book for you. I find purpose in sharing these life lessons that have served me and my clients so well over the years. All my other weights (responsibilities) are resting at my feet until this writing session is complete.

Right now, I am still Edward's wife and BabyGirl's Mama Patrice. I still have work responsibilities, a team I lead, and clients I serve. However, this moment is dedicated to you. You are my priority of the moment. Therefore, I am giving my full attention and full heart to this work right now. When my writing session is over, I'll save the document, shut down my computer and move on to family time. I will put my "author" weight down and pick up my "wife" weight. Then at some point later this evening, I'll lay all my weights down to get a good night's rest.

You see, the key to getting it all done is less about carrying all your weight at the same time and more about knowing how to make the exchange. If you're at work, keep your mind and emotions at work. This is the only way to ensure you're giving your best. If your workday is interrupted by a family emergency, lay that work weight down and respond to the needs of your family. Do not allow yourself to feel guilty about making the exchange. Guilt is a hindrance that produces nothing. If you give your best during the time you are at work, you have no reason to wallow in guilt for exchanging your work weight for your family weight or even for your self-care weight.

To give adequate care and attention to all your responsibilities, you must give yourself permission to make the exchange. Allow time and place to be your guide. If you are at work, be fully at work. Keep your focus at work. This may mean having a conversation with your family and friends about work boundaries. Help them understand what you need to minimize distractions at work so you can get things done and be free to enjoy them when you are at home.

When you get home, make good on that promise. Be wholly at home. This may mean resisting work email through the evening or setting boundaries with colleagues about the types of calls you will accept after hours. Communication is key. People appreciate knowing the boundaries, and those closest to you usually love you enough to respect them. The people who are bothered by your boundaries are the people you need them for most.

Let It Fall

We discussed earlier how your people may not offer support to you because you never look like you need support. You do everything in your power to make things work even if that effort is killing you. You make yourself the sacrificial lamb while frustration brews in your heart. Friend, sometimes you need to let it fall. Let it fail. Maybe you need to allow the project to fail so your company can see it was never appropriately funded. Maybe you need to allow the laundry to pile up for your family members to notice you've been taking care of it alone for too long. Maybe you need to allow your teenager

People will treat you how you train them to treat you.

to learn the hard way instead of exhausting your emotional and physical strength to save them from themselves.

Friend, I know it's hard to hear, but every now and then, you need to let it fall. When you have said what you can say and exhausted attempts at convincing, maybe people need to see for themselves. If you find yourself feeling misused and unappreciated, I challenge you to consider what you have taught people around you. People will treat you how you train them to treat you. If you always say yes, your people have learned to ask you first. If you never ask for help, your people have learned you don't need their help. If you always save the day, your people will expect you to put your cape on and get to work. What have you taught the people around you to expect from you? If everyone in your life depends on you, maybe you need to step back just enough for them to catch the slack.

What would happen if you stepped away for a bit? What would the people around you learn if you took your hands off the project? What if you were not the one to volunteer this time? What if you decided not to take one for the team again? What if you allowed the awkward silence until someone else stepped up? What if you gave a gracious no, making room for others to finally say yes? Every now and then, you need to let it fall.

Release the Emotion

Sometimes you just need to cry. How often have you tried to hold it together while your heart feels like it's about to explode? So many of us grew up in spaces where we learned crying was wrong or showed weakness. We were taught only babies cry, and beyond a certain age, tears are unacceptable. Statements like "Keep crying, and I'm gonna give you something to cry about!" taught us to hold back tears. In your adult life, people can get uncomfortable when they don't know how to hold space for your tears. So you learn to keep them in or keep them to yourself. Friend, God gave us a natural emotional release valve. He understood this life would be heavy sometimes, so in His infinite wisdom, He gave us a way to release. You need to cry.

Emotions are meant to be expressed. Like a pot of water on the stove, it may look like nothing is happening on the surface, but if you leave it on the fire long enough, it will boil over until it is empty and burned. How many times have you blown up on the wrong person because you were carrying unexpressed emotions? You are a human being with real emotions. The full spectrum of emotions is a consequence of a full life. Create a boundary that you will safely express your emotions as needed without holding back.

Now, Friend, don't pull a "Waiting to Exhale" and set the place on fire; I said safely. Identify a space and a person where you can safely release the valve. Prayer is a safe place. Find a good friend who has the capacity to honor your tears. Go to therapy. I know I said it before, but I will keep saying it. You need a place where you can release without concern for the feelings of any other person. Counseling is that place for many of us. Decide that you will allow your heart to speak. Cry when you need to cry.

Create Margin for Rest

You need a margin for rest. A margin is the border or boundary nothing should cross. Like the margin of lined paper, all the details should be inside the margin and the space beyond the margin should be blank. You need blank time when nothing is scheduled and your soul can rest.

When I mention rest, most of my clients fall back on "I don't have time." Friend, you do not wait on time to rest. You create time to rest. Rest is not a reward; rest is a requirement. There are three types of rest you should implement: selah, sabbath, and sabbatical.

You find the word selah[4] throughout the book of Psalms. A technical term from music, it means to stop and think about what was just spoken. It also means pause, interrupt, rest, or silence. The Bible uses this term to encourage you to be thoughtful as you reflect on the Psalms. I use the term to describe the type of rest you need daily. Selah rest is taking three to thirty minutes throughout your day to get some fresh air, take a walk, breathe, pray, or just be silent.

You may think you can only rest if you're on a tropical island somewhere drinking a—whatever you choose. Friend, that's your business, but I'm here to tell you it's possible for you to recover your rest even in the midst of crazy workdays. Schedule in your selah time. You plan everything else that's important to you. Plan your rest. Give yourself some cushion between meetings. Schedule thirty minutes of selah before a tough meeting. Use your lunch time to recharge instead of checking email. Get away from your desk and get outside. Feel the breeze on your cheek. Breathe fresh air.

My sister-friend Jemekka Richardson would tell you to get some car therapy. Go to your car, turn on soothing music, lay the seat back, and just be. Take ten minutes during the workday or fifteen minutes in your driveway and allow your car to be your refuge. Use small chunks of time throughout your day to engage your vagus nerve and bring calm to your spirit. You'll return more productive and creative after a small amount of intentional rest.

You also need sabbath rest. Sabbath[5][6] refers to *a day* set aside for rest and recovery. The term means to cease and desist or to rest.

You need one day per week set aside for rest, worship, and play. One day away from the email. One day away from responsibilities. One day away from news cycles and the troubles of the world. You need one day to reboot your system after the stress of an entire week.

To learn more about the power of sabbath, I encourage you to read *The Ruthless Elimination of Hurry*, by John Mark Comer, and *Obedience over Hustle*, by Malinda Fuller. As a result of these books, my family and I take at least one day per week just to rest, worship, and play. This worship is not about serving at church either, Friend. For folks who serve in ministry, your church day is not your rest day. You need a day apart from your obligations at work, church, and in the community just to commune with God and with your immediate family members. Go on a hike. Enjoy ice cream. Dive into a swimming pool. Dance. Put all your tech away and just be for one day.

Finally, you need sabbatical rest. The word sabbatical is related to the word sabbath; it also means rest. This term is often used in academic settings when faculty members travel away from their home institution for the sake of research. This time away offers them an opportunity to focus on their research interest without the normal competing priorities of teaching and institutional service.

Sabbatical rest is a break or change from your routine. In her *Forbes* article "The Untold Value of a Professional Sabbatical," Tamara Schwarting writes, "The purpose of a sabbatical is to give an employee a chance to step back from their role at work and focus on personal enrichment and professional development."[7] When was the last time you stepped away for personal enrichment and professional development?

As a young leader, I made the mistake of dedicating all the professional development money to my team members while I stayed on campus to cover for them. Although noble, this was not a wise leadership decision. After a long hiatus from traveling, I finally took an opportunity to present at a conference. Returning from the conference refreshed and renewed, I vowed I would never delay my own professional development that long again.

Friend, sabbatical rest creates separation between you and your normal environment. Getting away allows your mind to rest and gives you a fresh perspective on your projects, goals, and challenges. Just taking a day off is not the same as a sabbatical. Sitting at home, you may still be surrounded by your responsibilities. You may not be working, but you're still grinding in your head, thinking of all the things you should be doing. A physical separation gives you permission to temporarily leave it all behind.

If your employer doesn't offer official sabbatical leave for your role, find ways to take a week or more away. Take a cruise, and don't pay for the internet package. Attend a personal development conference where you have no responsibilities. Go on a wellness retreat. Have a staycation at a local hotel, and act like a tourist in your own city. Participate in a virtual retreat, but connect to the meeting from a local hotel lobby or co-working space. Go to a ministry conference where no one knows who you are or what you do. Get out of your normal environment for more than one day to recharge and refuel.

Reclaim Your Time

In her book, *Overwhelmed: Work, Love, and Play When No One Has the Time*, Brigid Schulte introduces the term time confetti.[8] Schulte describes time confetti as the act of losing volumes of time, second by second. Schulte explains how our time escapes us in bite-sized increments. One quick email or a two-minute scroll multiplied by several times a day equates to losing several precious minutes of time per day to mindless, useless activity. As we all proclaim we don't have time for self-care or other important things, somehow, we find time to waste during our days. It seems innocent enough, one minute here or five minutes there, but before you know it, thirty minutes to an hour has passed, and your mind is more cluttered than it was before you wandered off.

Reclaim your time. Gather the two-minute and five-minute increments back to you and repurpose them for good. Use that time for your selah rest. How refreshed would you be if you took twelve minutes a day to walk outdoors instead of doom scrolling through your phone? Not only would you protect yourself from more bad news, but you would also add some body movement, fresh air, and a small break from looking at screens.

You don't need large chunks of time to recover. Take your time scraps and put them together to create a good moment of reprieve in your day. No one can create more time, but everyone can become a better steward of the time we have.

Friend, these boundaries work for me, but you need boundaries specifically suited for your life. Use these suggestions as a starting place to determine what boundaries you need. Building walls around your soul protects the brilliance God created in you. Do not roam around vulnerable, and do not wait for someone else to provide your protection. You are your first advocate. Protect what means most to you by building boundaries that work.

Do the Heart Work

Confess this: Anything that will serve me well for the rest of my life is worth temporary sacrifice.

Test Your Boundaries

1. Choose one boundary from this chapter that connects to your values. Decide how you will implement the boundary in your life.
2. Test that new boundary for one week. Note what worked about the boundary and what did not work.
3. Revise your action plan and test that same boundary again the next week.
4. Tweak and change until you feel adequately protected in that area.

Chapter 10

Discover Your Brilliance

In August 2022, I had the opportunity to visit Idaho State University for the first time. I decided to arrive on campus early so I could find a parking spot and the room where I would give my presentation. As I wandered through the building, looking for the right room, I almost walked right into a woman who exclaimed, "Dr. PBJ, is that you?!" I said "Yes!" with great relief and asked, "Did they send you to find me?" She said, "Nope, but I can show you to your room."

As this professor walked me to my room, I shared my gratitude that I had run into her. She told me how she often finds herself in position to help people find their way. She points people in the right direction on campus and in grocery stores. On a trip to Disney World, a family stepped off the tram, ignored every Disney cast member dressed in staff uniforms, and came straight to her to inquire how to find the castle. This professor responded by pulling out an extra map from her fanny pack, drawing a path from the tram to the castle, and handing that map over to the grateful family.

I was so excited to hear her story as I was preparing to speak with this group of faculty members about discovering their brilliance. I looked her straight in her eyes and asked if she realized she was more than a professor. "You don't just teach sociology. You help lost people find their way. When students come to your classroom, they don't just come to learn. They come to find their way." Her eyes filled with tears as she whispered, "I never thought about it that way." Brilliance was always there. She just needed someone to hold up a mirror so she could see it.

And the same is true for you. Your brilliance is not hidden. You just need a little help discovering it. In that process, you're seeking to identify your innate, unique brilliance so you may fulfill the calling of God on your life. You're fed up with aimless grinding and ready to embrace the value you innately bring to the world.

These are some of the milestones you'll hit as you discover your brilliance:

- Understand the difference between your skills, talents, passion(s) and your purpose.
- Identify your purpose apart from your career title and your job description.
- Clearly and concisely articulate the value you bring to the world without doubt or confusion.

In discovering your brilliance, you will be enlightened by recognizing all the ways purpose has manifested in your life, and you will be ignited by new opportunities to walk wholly in brilliance.

Hurdles to Discovering Brilliance

"How do I find my purpose?" This is the question I most frequently receive in my inbox. Before I walk you through the steps of discovering and living in your brilliance, I need you to know what stands in the way of this discovery. After checking your backpack and building strong boundaries, I've found three primary hurdles to discovering brilliance: (1) Western culture promotes work over purpose; (2) you think you have to start all over; and (3) you believe purpose must be difficult to be valuable.

In American culture, we often ask children, "What do you want to be when you grow up?" As soon as a child is old enough to attend school, they're constantly confronted with this question. If we're honest, we're not asking about their being. We're really asking, "What do you want to do for a job when you grow up?" This conversation continues into adulthood. When we meet a new person, early in the conversation, we often ask, "What do you do?"

These questions condition us to focus on our doing instead of our being. What if instead of asking a child what they want to be when they grow up, we studied them to notice how God shaped them? Proverbs 22:6 teaches us to "Train up a child in the way he should go: and when he is old, he will not depart from it." In the original Hebrew language, this verse means to guide your child toward their natural bent; toward the purpose they were created to fulfill. In other words, we should steer our children toward their brilliance, not toward any specific career.

All is not lost if you didn't have anyone in your life with the awareness to steer you toward brilliance as a child. It's not too late for you to investigate your life to find the breadcrumbs of brilliance along your path. Just like you should study your children and grandchildren to identify their natural, God-given brilliance, I encourage you to look back over your own life to discover how the fingerprints of God have always been on your life. The purpose of discovering your brilliance is to reconnect with the Father's original intention for your life. He had a plan for you before you took your first breath. It is time for you to recognize that plan and align your life with it. You are about to discover your being and release the unnecessary doing.

The second common barrier to your brilliance is your fear of stepping forward because you think you'll have to start over. When I began to see my brilliance, I couldn't deny the revelation, but I tried to avoid it. I thought I would have to start all over. *You mean to tell me I've invested twenty years of my life into a career, and now I'm going to walk away from it?* I was so attached to my doing that I couldn't see the gift has been the same all along. Walking into brilliance did require me to let go of many things, but one of the greatest lessons I learned is it did not require me to start over.

Your brilliance will build on everything you've built so far. Everything I'm doing now was built upon those twenty years of learning and relationship building. Brilliance will not require you to throw it all away. Brilliance will honor where you've been and take you to where you are supposed to be.

The final barrier to address is your belief that purpose must be difficult to be valuable. You fail to place value on the brilliance inside you because it feels too easy to be valuable. It comes easy to you, so you think it must be easy for everyone. Friend, the brilliance that flows so easily from you is like climbing the highest mountain for another person. We are all a part of the same spiritual body, but each person has a distinct, unique part to fulfill (1 Corinthians 12:12-27). Your brilliance flows freely from you with little effort. You expressed the same brilliance as a child that you're longing for now. God created you with a supernatural ability to express a specific brilliance that does not require performance. Friend, your brilliance comes easy to you.

I'll walk you through this process of discovering your brilliance and living in it. As we do this work, our ultimate goal is for you to ensure that every passion and action in your life aligns with your brilliance. Discovering your brilliance relieves the conflict of misalignment in your soul and frees you from the Cycle of Burnout. The best news is free people free other people, so get ready to make an impact!

The Blessing is in the Seeking

Brilliance is not a pinnacle you reach one day after a lifetime of searching. Discovering your brilliance is not an ending; it is a journey. Do not expect to cross a finish line or make it to a pinnacle of completion. Most people who come to me seeking support in finding purpose expect to discover a secret code that gives them their purpose and then live happily ever after. Friend, what you are going to find is a path specifically ordered for you by God. The blessing is not in the completion. The blessing is in the seeking.

Consider how Jesus taught about the kingdom of God while He walked the earth. Jesus often taught through parables, simple stories used to share deep truths. In Matthew 13:10-13, the disciples asked Jesus why he used parables.

His disciples came and asked him, "Why do you use parables when you talk to the people?"

He replied, "You are permitted to understand the secrets of the Kingdom of Heaven, but others are not. To those who listen to my teaching, more understanding will be given, and they will have an abundance of knowledge. But for those who are not listening, even what little understanding they have will be taken away from them. That is why I use these parables,

> For they look, but they don't really see.
> They hear, but they don't really listen or understand."

The keys of the Kingdom of God are for seekers only, those who will listen, study, and submit to the will of the Lord. The more you tune in, the more you will understand. The more you seek, the more you will find. Your seeking is not in vain. There is a promise stated in Matthew 7:7-8 that guarantees the outcome of your seeking:

> "Keep on asking, and you will receive what you ask for. Keep on seeking, and you will find. Keep on knocking, and the door will be opened to you. For everyone who asks, receives. Everyone who seeks, finds. And to everyone who knocks, the door will be opened."

God promised to reveal His truth to seekers, so the real power is in the seeking, not the knowing. Get curious about God and His Word. Get curious about who He created you to be. Please note I said get curious, not get anxious. Trust God enough to obey the step for today without knowing the step for tomorrow. Release the pressure to know the entire plan. That is not how God leads us. He is a step-by-step God. Read scripture. Ask questions. Journal. Pray. Seek.

Matthew, one of Jesus's disciples, instructs us to seek the kingdom of God first, before anything else, and everything else we need will be added to us (Matthew 6:33). God has not called us to seek because He's hiding something from us. We need to seek because He hides kingdom keys *for* us—for our benefit. It's the greatest treasure hunt of all time! He knows the seeking will lead to greater wisdom, new skills, deeper levels of understanding, sharpening of your soul, a thicker skin, transformational relationships, and a new level of fulfillment at each new level of brilliance. God instructs us to seek because we receive everything we need with each step we take.

The Father will not ask you to do anything He doesn't do. God is a seeker. Jesus told of a woman who had ten silver coins but lost one (Luke 15:8-10). She swept her whole house and turned it upside down to find that coin. When she found it, she rejoiced with her friends. In the same chapter, we learn of a shepherd who had one hundred sheep but lost one (Luke 15:3-7). Jesus told how the shepherd left the ninety-nine to go find the one and rejoiced with his friends when the sheep was recovered. Both parables show how significant each person is to God.

God is not satisfied with good enough. No matter how many of His children are with Him, His heart is always seeking the one who is lost. We erroneously believe we found God. The truth is He found us. He sought after us until we were found. According to John 4:23, the Father is seeking people who will worship Him in

Spirit and in truth. God expects us to seek because He himself is a seeker. Seek God. Seek your brilliance.

Brilliance Evolves

As you walk in brilliance, you will become increasingly acquainted with the depth of your innate, unique gift. The more I allowed God to use me as a crisis disruptor, the more I began to see my brilliance is more than that. God has given me a supernatural ability to hear what's not said and a voice that brings healing. My coaching clients often experience breakthroughs as I reflect to them feelings and values they never expressed in words. I can hear beyond the words. I hear the longings of the heart. By holding up this mirror, I empower my clients to address a side of their story that was hidden.

Folks who listen to my podcast often remark on the soothing nature of my voice. I never thought there was anything special about my voice until I started the podcast, but many people over the years have shared how my voice brings comfort and healing to them. I am now aware that God gave me my voice as a balm for those who are hurting. I am intentional about the words I speak and how I use my voice as I now see how brilliance flows through my instrument.

Dr. Sasha had recently completed her doctoral work when she joined our coaching community. She had worked as a counselor for many years and was established in the field, but she struggled to see the core of her brilliance. She knew she wasn't defined by her work, but she desperately desired to identify the gift of God inside her. Through the HeartWork strategies, Sasha uncovered an innate, unique gift for teaching. Although she had never had the title of teacher, she had been a trainer on multiple jobs. She served as the onboarding trainer at her counseling firm, and she even taught dance to children at church. Through HeartWork, she began to see how the light in her life shone over the years through her teaching.

Over the course of our time together, Sasha was offered and accepted an opportunity to become a full-time professor, moving from counseling full time to training new counselors. Our community had the honor of supporting her as she said goodbye to colleagues and a profession she had invested in for years and stepped into her next adventure. Sasha has discovered the joy of living in brilliance every day and remains connected to the HeartWork Community as her brilliance evolves.

There are layers of your brilliance you cannot access until you walk in it. Through discovering brilliance, you become aware of your innate, unique gift, and as you live in brilliance, you are exposed to the breadth and depth of power given to you by our Heavenly Father. You are His child, and as such, you resemble your Father. As you discover the vastness of His love for you, you will also discover the colors, textures, and power of the brilliance He gave you to sow into the earth.

Brilliance Requires Laser Focus

To produce the most impact, your brilliance should be focused as directed by God. As you walk more fully in your brilliance, more people will see your shine. This causes people to be drawn to you and your gift like a magnet. You will receive offers and opportunities you didn't ask for or expect. Do not, I repeat, *do not* be dazzled by an offer. Do not be intoxicated by the attention. Approach every door prayerfully and soberly. Practice obeying God in small things so you will hear Him clearly concerning the big things.

Ask questions like:

- God, should I call this person back?
- Is this assignment something you want me to do?
- Is this the place you would have me invest my gift?
- Father, is this opportunity within your will for my life?
- Do I have your endorsement on this opportunity?
- Father, will you please show me anything on my plate you didn't assign to my hands?

Pastor Dharius Daniels of Change Church shared three powerful lessons about remaining focused within the plan of God for your life in his sermon *This is Confusing//Stranger Things Part. 2*.[1] He proclaimed these three lessons allowed him "to reach [his] goals without destroying [his] soul".

- "Just because I am able to doesn't mean I'm assigned to."
- "Saying yes to the wrong thing means you will have to say no to the right thing."
- "God never withholds something from you and gives you something inferior in return."

Climbing the ladder of success without the focus of the Father who created you will lead you to destruction. There is no gold-star system or 4.0 to obtain. The Father made you for your brilliance, and He promised not to "lay anything heavy or ill-fitting on you" (Matthew 11:30[MSG]). He knows how you should express your brilliance and where that brilliance is best applied. Ask the Father. Focus only on what He requires of you. Do only what He says. Doing more than He says is not impressive. It's disobedient. Trust Him to keep you focused.

Skills, Talents, Passions, and Purpose

To discover your brilliance, you must understand the difference between your skills, talents, passions, and purpose. One of the dangers of being an incredibly capable woman is that you can do a lot of things. Many women find themselves in burnout because they spend most of their life focused on skills and talents that drain their energy and for which they have no intrinsic motivation. Again, just because you can do it does not mean you should. Making a shift to focus on purpose and passion provides the greatest impact from you and ignites an intrinsic fire that cannot be contained.

Skills are tasks you've been trained to do, but if you're honest, you can admit you're not very good at them. You can get the job done, but you struggle. Skills cost you greatly in time, attention, effort, and emotion because they don't flow freely from you. You must exert a lot of energy to complete the tasks. As an example, in higher education we have very intricate budget processes. Now, Friend, I was trained in these processes every year for twenty years, but I had to relearn them every time budget season came around. I got the job done, and I never got my hand slapped because of a budget error, but it cost me an excessive amount of time, tears, and frustration every single year. Budget season demanded about a week locked in my office for hours, trying to wrap my mind around all the steps. It's just not my thing. These tedious processes do not come naturally to me. I did them, but, man, was it difficult.

A skill may be a requirement of your job, but if you could delegate it, that task would be the first thing you'd hire someone else to do. You cannot ignore your skills because they are often a necessary part of your work, but if all your time is spent focused on skills, you will be eternally exhausted and dread the thought of each new day.

Grab your *Disrupting Burnout* journal. It's time to identify your skills. What tasks have you learned to do (because you had to) that you're not good at? Which tasks or responsibilities drain every ounce of motivation out of you? List at least 3 of your skills.

Next, consider your talents. Unlike skills, you're pretty good at your talents. You are probably better than many other people in these areas. You may have been recognized or complimented for having the talent, but if you're honest, it still costs you an extreme amount of energy to get things done in that area. You accomplish the task exceptionally well, but you're not motivated to do it very often.

Talents are risky business for professional women because this can be a place where you get stuck. People who recognize your talent want you to do that task all the time because you're so good at it. That's just human nature on their part. So you settle. You settle for good enough. You settle for the pat on the back. You settle for the validation. You settle for the achievement. But you know there's more. Your heart is exhausted at the thought of having to do it too much longer. You are good at it, but it still costs you time, effort, attention, and emotion.

I have a talent for working through techy things, like building my own website, editing my videos, and running my social media. An IT expert may call me out as a fraud, but to the untrained eye, I'm pretty good. There's even a bit of enjoyment in it for me. I feel accomplished after I've tinkered long enough to figure out new software. But the truth is it takes me too much time to accomplish a small techy task that an expert could get done in a matter of minutes. It costs me days and mental energy to take care of tech tasks in my business, and I often fail to get it right on the first try. When I compare my tech abilities to other tech novices, I rank top of the class, but no one is calling on me to fix their computer—well, except my husband and my mama. I will never be known as a tech expert, but I have done well enough at it to run my business. I call that a talent.

I also have a talent for cooking. Well, we should be clear. I make a few things that are home runs every time. Crockpot mac and cheese, red velvet cake, and 7-up cake are my most popular requests. I have to say my red velvet cake is unmatched. I have yet to taste one better, and those who have tasted my cake over the years agree. Everything else I cook is average, or maybe slightly above, but my cakes and mac and cheese stand above the rest.

I fell in love with cooking through my Granma Ozella. She was the manager of the cafeteria in our local high school and believed in sharing love through food. She and I cooked together every Saturday for many years in my childhood—homemade biscuits, apple pie, and our specialty, gooey bars. Gooey bars are my workplace potluck fan favorite. I would tell you what's in them, but I am sworn to secrecy. My colleagues have tried to get that recipe out of me for years, but I promised Granma to only share it with my daughter. (Google "gooey butter cake." It's the closest I've found.)

I enjoy cooking, but it's a talent, not a passion or purpose for me. Some people cook big dinners and complicated desserts on a regular basis for fun. They experiment and try their own mix of ingredients to create masterpieces. I use recipes; a real cook may say that's blasphemy. I rarely make the red velvet cake because it's such a laborious recipe. I get rave reviews every time I make it, but the effort is a bit excessive for me. All these favorites listed above only come out for the holidays; your girl is not cooking up red velvet cakes on any random Tuesday. It's a talent. I am better than many when it comes to cooking, but the effort wears me out.

What are your talents? When I asked this question during a workshop recently, three of the ladies identified party planning as their talent. They get called on to plan family events, and they're good at it, but they would rather not do it. They try to hide from it, but they get called on every time.

What are some things you're good at (better than many) but which you'd rather not do too often? List those talents in your journal.

Passion vs. Purpose

Passion and purpose are where you want to invest most of your time, attention, emotion, and effort. I use purpose and brilliance interchangeably; they are the same. In Christian communities, we also use the word "calling" to describe purpose and brilliance. Many people mistake a passion for their purpose. Passion and purpose are often used interchangeably, but they are not the same.

Purpose is the innate, unique brilliance you bring to the world. Passion is an expression of your brilliance, the way you share your brilliance with the world. Failure to understand the difference contributed significantly to my burnout. Passion is fiery, reckless, and intense. Purpose brings structure and boundaries to your passions.

Without purpose, chasing passions will drive you into burnout. Without purpose, you think you must do all things to pursue your passion instead of being who you were created to be and doing what flows easily from you. For example, I'm passionate about education. I truly believe education changed the trajectory of my life and the lives of generations to come after me. Therefore, I dedicated my life to education. I'm great at it and I believe in it. And my passion for education drove me to a breaking point.

Because I thought I was operating in purpose, I didn't know how to say no. I failed to build boundaries because I thought education was my ultimate calling. I learned the hard way that passion is more about doing and purpose is about being. Passion is the expression of purpose. Passion is how I share my purpose with the world through my gifts, like teaching, speaking, writing, and singing.

You may be passionate about many things, but they all flow from one purpose. Every passion is birthed from your innate, unique brilliance. Purpose is your being. Passion is the vehicle through which purpose is presented; it is your doing. Making the transition from exhausting passion to living in brilliance freed me to serve well without paying irreversible consequences. Purpose-filled women clearly distinguish between their purpose and their passions, allowing their brilliance to be their guide.

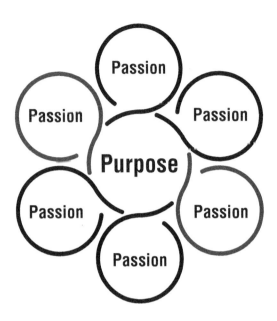

The graphic above shows how you have one purpose — one innate, unique brilliance. That brilliance is expressed through several passions—jobs, roles, accomplishments, behaviors, acts, and service. Most people I've met have trouble pinpointing their purpose right away, because we have not been taught to value our being over our doing. Therefore, to discover your brilliance it is often useful to start by considering your passions.

> Complete the Purpose vs. Passion diagram in your *Disrupting Burnout* journal using the instructions below. First, fill in the outer circles with all your passions.

Think about the things you've done throughout your life—jobs, volunteer opportunities, family roles, performances, and other activities. Don't just consider experiences you find applaudable. Add your very first job and your leadership roles in college. Remember the ways you showed up in school. Consider your role(s) in group projects and friend groups. Recount your position as a student athlete or captain of the debate team. In what ways have you volunteered or offered service without payment? Brilliance is not just connected to what you get paid to do. Brilliance shows up in every aspect of your life. Don't limit your thoughts to accolades or high-profile wins. Brilliance did not show up the first day you were recognized for something good. You've been brilliant since your first breath.

After documenting as many expressions as you can remember, think about your impact.

1. What were the outcomes or benefits *for others* of you serving in each role?
2. What were the outcomes or benefits *for you* serving in each role?
3. What do these outcomes and benefits have in common?
4. What themes do you find among the list of impacts?
5. What is the one common thread that flows through each experience?

We will chat more about connecting the dots in the next section. No pressure to have the right answer, Friend. This is an activity you will revisit as you become more familiar with your brilliance. Our goal in this moment is for you to awaken to awareness of your own brilliance.

Purpose and Passion in Action

I'm encouraged by powerful women who identify their purpose from their passions. I watched a video of Oprah Winfrey speaking at the Stanford Graduate School of Business. When asked about purpose, Oprah says, "It looks like I was a talk show host. It looks like I was in the movies. It looks like I own a network. But my real contribution is to help connect people to themselves and the higher ideas of consciousness. I'm here to help raise consciousness." [2]

Oprah clearly separates her being from her doing. Her brilliance (purpose) is connecting people to ideas and stories so they can live a better life. She has expressed that brilliance (passions) through a talk show and the OWN network, through acting in movies, by opening a school for girls in South Africa, and in many other ways. As much as Oprah Winfrey has accomplished, she does not define herself by the doing. She's clear on her brilliance, which fuels the impact of her passions.

Tunde Oyeneyin is a Peloton instructor, Nike athlete, and author of the *New York Times* bestseller *Speak.* Tunde shares in her memoir her path from losing a significant amount of weight in high school to selling department store makeup and to all the accolades she enjoys today. Tunde writes that she "helps people discover themselves for the first time." This brilliance is not something new. It didn't emerge after she was chosen for the national stage that is Peloton. Throughout her story, there's a consistent thread of helping people discover themselves for the first time, which she expressed through her passions for makeup, exercise, speaking, writing, and empowering. Tunde understands if she left Peloton tomorrow, the innate, unique brilliance she brings to the world would not end. Her current international stage with Peloton is a vehicle for her purpose, not the purpose itself.[3]

Serena Williams, arguably the best tennis player in the world to-date, is more than that. One might assume tennis had to be her purpose because she was such a prominent figure in that world and so skilled at the sport. Tennis is a passion, a powerful vehicle through which she has shared her purpose with the world. However, to walk away with such grace, Serena must understand that she's more than tennis.

I continue to watch her journey as she expands her foray into entrepreneurship and focuses on motherhood. Serena Williams has an undeniable will to win like none other. In an interview with the team at Slack, Serena explains she requires honest feedback from every person on her team, from her nutritionist to her stylist. "When pressed about why constructive criticism is so important to her, she offers a pragmatic answer. 'There's someone working just as hard as me, if not harder. They're trying to beat me, and I need to always stay a step above.'"[4]

In another interview, she discusses her absolute disdain for losing. This supernatural competitive edge is not siloed to tennis; it impacts every aspect of her life. Whether she is designing new fashion or starring in commercials, I know we'll continue to be impacted by her innate, unique brilliance, her competitive spirit.

A news story in the "On the Road" segment, by Steve Hartman, on *CBS Evening News*, on April 7, 2023, perfectly shows how your brilliance is not limited by your job title or job description. The students at Weatherbee Elementary in Hampden, Maine, became the state chess champions due to the brilliance of their coach. School custodian David Bishop heard the children practicing their chess moves one day after school and couldn't help but join the fun.

Mr. Bishop had played the game since his childhood and simply loved it. He had no background in teaching and had never been trained to teach the game. But did you notice his name? *Mr. Bishop*? He was made for this! With guidance and coaching from

Mr. Bishop, the students went from unknown to state champions. When asked about his role in the win, Mr. Bishop says, "When they told me to make the school shine, they never said how." Oh, I love that so much!

Mr. Bishop was not stifled by his title, level, or job description. He didn't paralyze himself with thoughts of "That's not my job." David Bishop found new joy at work and his avenue to shine through an innate, unique brilliance only he could provide to the students. The segment ends with Mr. Bishop saying, "I found my purpose." Have you found your purpose, Friend? Do you know who you are beyond the title, salary, and job description? It's time to discover your brilliance.[5]

Connect the Dots

Brilliance is in you now and has been for your entire life. To discover your innate, unique brilliance, you only need to trace your own steps. Connect the dots. Travel back through your experiences and mark your impact. What do you find in common among all the ways you have impacted the world? Through this exercise, my business bestie Dr. Raymona Lawrence, found a theme of recognizing and implementing systems to ensure a project, organization, or body works efficiently. When I introduced this process to my sister-friend Tiesha Andrews, she found a theme of guiding people toward light in their lives. My impact theme is walking folks through crisis. Allow me to share my own walk with you as an example of the journey.

Friends and Family. I have always been the person you call on your worst day. My phone rarely rings for casual conversation or with an invite to go shopping. Normally, when my phone rings, someone needs something. They're hurt. They're upset. They may be crying. This has been true all my life. Adults came to me with their problems when I was a child. I once told a lady, "Ma'am, I'm twelve. I don't know what to do about your marriage, but I can listen." I was the big sister extraordinaire, caring for my brother and sister like they were my own. I have always been the person you lean on when your strength is gone. I am the person you call when you don't know what else to do or who else to call. I get down into your crisis with you and help you walk through it.

Profession. I was on call for over twenty years, which means I responded to crisis calls at all times of the day or night. As a young professional, I lived in the residence halls with college students, so they only had to knock on my door. They knocked for everything from needing toilet paper to needing help with a friend struggling with suicidal ideation.

As I developed in my career, I moved off campus, but the on-call responsibilities remained. As a mid-level professional, it was my job to coach my team through lower-level crisis situations and to lead through life-threatening or life-altering situations. I responded in person if a student was arrested, hospitalized, or victimized. As an executive leader, my on-call responsibilities were mostly coaching, but the occasional flood in the residence hall or student tragedy demanded my attention. In addition to serving on call, my daily responsibilities included any number of student concerns, complaints, and crises.

Ministry. In ministry with my husband, my role continues to be the crisis support person. I tend to gravitate to the moments when someone needs a hug or they need someone to stand with them on their hardest day. I have supported several laboring moms in the delivery room and stood with many people as they buried loved ones. There have been many coffee dates full of tears and even more tearful phone calls. My heart is bent toward people suffering in one way or another.

Research. On the day we lost our five nursing students, I was in the process of writing a dissertation on the role of the dean of students in managing campus crisis. I spent four years conducting research around the subject of crisis management before I had any idea about my personal brilliance.

Coaching. When I transitioned out of traditional higher education work, I moved into a space where I support teams and individual professionals through disrupting burnout and other cycles that hamper productivity and collective brilliance. Teams in crisis bring me in to equip and support them in walking out of that crisis and into productive purpose. And now, I'm walking with you as you gather the tools to beat burnout so you can know and maximize your brilliance.

Friend, I am the crisis buster. It's just who I am. I help you see beyond your current struggle to the light of a better tomorrow. When I look back over my journey, this is what I've always done. No matter the job title or job description, when you call on PBJ, someone in the room needs to know there is brilliance in them and tomorrow will be a better day. This is my brilliance.

Take some time now to connect your dots. What do you find when you consider the ways you have expressed brilliance throughout your life? Wander back through your life experiences to find your common thread of impact.

As you think through your jobs, roles, and responsibilities, what difference have you made? It may be helpful here to chat with family and friends. Ask them how they see your role in the family or friend group. Ask them what impact you've had in their life. Do not challenge their responses; just listen and take notes. Receive every compliment and let it land. Allow your people to help you identify your brilliance.

Do the HeartWork

Let's take this one step further. Remember your brilliance is not just about your doing, but it's more about your being. Your brilliance is your identity; it's your superpower. You need to look beyond jobs, roles, and responsibilities to discover your brilliance. Take some time to journal through the following questions. This activity should not be timed. As a matter of fact, I encourage you not to do this in one sitting. Visit and revisit the following questions as you journey through your life in search of your brilliance. Look for light. As you answer the questions, look for themes that continue to show up along your path. Note the commonalities as you go. What clues do you find concerning the brilliance God placed in you? Take your time. Enjoy this journey.

 Download the *Disrupting Burnout* journal for a fillable copy of this activity at patricebuckner jackson.com/journal or scan the QR code for access.

Here are a few things to keep in mind as you do this HeartWork:

- Pray before you begin. Ask Holy Spirit to help you see the light of God inside you. Let Him know you trust Him to reveal what you need to see.

- Feel free to write, video record, or audio record your responses. Use the most comfortable method for you. Do not allow the recording method to be a hindrance.
- There are no right or wrong answers. Just document what comes to your mind with each question.
- Do not critique your thoughts and do not leave anything out. Note everything that comes to mind.
- Do not allow the burden of other people's opinions to rob you of this experience.
- Do not skip questions. There's significance in every step. The step you skip may hold the clarity you seek.

Record your answers to the following questions:

1. What is the most impactful compliment you've ever received? Why is this compliment so significant to you?
2. What is a compliment you receive often?
3. Who were you as a child?
   a. What did you care about?
   b. What frustrated you?
   c. What did you get in trouble for?
   d. What made you happy?
   e. What were your struggles?
6. What life events have shaped who you are?
7. What role(s) do you fill for family and friends? What do they depend on you for?
8. What accomplishment are you most proud of and why?
9. What are your favorite volunteer or community service activities? Why is this work so significant to you?

10. What work experiences gave or give you the most fulfillment? Think back to your very first job and up until now.

11. What would you do with your life if money wasn't a concern and the opinions of others didn't matter?

12. What patterns do you see in your responses to the questions above? What stands out to you as you review your path?

Friend, you do not have to look for purpose because your purpose is not lost. Brilliance has been in you for your entire life; this is just an opportunity for you to recognize it. You will never discover brilliance outside of yourself. Everything you need is tucked into your own story. Invest the time to investigate your life so you can meet the woman God created you to be.

Chapter 11

Living in Brilliance

After leaving my executive position in August 2019 due to burnout, I spent five months at home with no job. Those months offered me a gift; I had time to think and dream like never before. During those five months, God spoke to me concerning the next season of my life. I'd always held a dream in my heart to travel and speak, but I assumed this dream was unrealistic. Until then, I'd limited the thought to "maybe one day after retirement." Burnout, however, caused me to surrender. I surrendered the plans I had for my life in exchange for God's plan. I surrendered my expectations for my career to grab hold of purpose, and I surrendered my fear of what other people might think of me. That last one is a stronghold I continue to surrender every day.

One of the factors that pushed me further into surrender was the consequences of leaving my job with no notice. As soon as word got out that I was available for hire, calls started coming in. Universities in my state were interested in hiring me. However, it wasn't long before the calls trailed away to nothing. Several administrators reached out with great excitement at first, and then I never heard from them again.

In speaking with some leaders in my field, I learned I had been blackballed. A trusted source told me anyone in the state with any interest in hiring me was quickly instructed that they were not to hire me by any means. Even folks I'd once considered mentors no longer took my calls. It wasn't fair, but I understood why. All those people were fearful for their own jobs. Advocating for me was a risk they were not willing to take.

I know my career field, and I know the way I left is considered unacceptable. So I wasn't angry, but I was concerned for my future. *What am I supposed to do now? Did I just ruin my entire life? Did I lose everything I worked so hard to build over the last twenty years?* I was forced to think outside of the box and consider if I could do something different. For the first time in my adult life, I was open to anything. This was my Crisis of Brilliance.

During this time of surrender, God stirred up my dream of becoming a full-time speaker. I remembered a prophecy I'd received when I was a child that I would speak all over the world. The prophet said people would be drawn to the love of Christ by my smile. Suddenly, I could imagine myself traveling and speaking all over the country. I had no idea where to start, but this dream would not leave me alone. I built a website and created a mission statement. At that point, I had no idea what I would speak about, but that website became my dream board. I tweaked and edited and tested ideas through it.

Before long, I began recording videos on my phone and writing blogs. I honestly didn't think it was worth much at the time. I was just doing what I felt in my heart I was supposed to do. Just doing the next thing. I trusted God to lead me to where I was supposed to be next. There's an old saying that you never know God is all you need until God is all you have. This is my testimony. I felt like I had this little dream lying dormant in a dusty corner of my heart, and during this time of reflection, God pulled that dream out of its hiding spot and doused it with passion fuel, and it began to blaze.

I wrote everything I heard and saw. It didn't make much sense at the time, but when I look at those notes now, I can see how God brought it all together. The more time I spent in prayer, therapy, and coaching, the clearer my brilliance became. There was no doubt in my mind that I am created to support people and teams through their crises. I just didn't know what to do with this brilliance.

I reminded myself that God is my source and any job or business He gives me is a resource. I renewed my trust in my Source. And He came through in a major way! Prior to my leaving my VP position in August 2019, Edward felt a need for us to save money. He's naturally a saver, but this was something different. He felt like we needed to be extravagant in our savings. I assumed this may be for a future dream home, so I agreed—although reluctantly at times. I'm so glad I listened. The money we saved in those ten months leading up to my resignation carried us until I received my first paycheck from my next full-time position in January 2020. We had just enough left to move to a new city and rent an apartment when I received the offer letter.

I was determined to give my best to this new position. Leadership had put their own names on the line to hire me. When others ran away, these leaders spoke up for me and pushed back against negative talk about me. Remember the president who I told, "I was born for this" in the middle of a crisis? He remembered. He remembered my work prior to that August day in 2019 and supported his team in hiring me regardless of what anyone had to say. I'm grateful for people who remember.

In my new position, I served as associate vice president for student affairs. I surrendered the executive cabinet position to embrace a middle-leadership position where my brilliance could shine. In this new role, I had daily contact with students, direct responsibility for training and coaching staff, and extensive crisis management responsibilities. Oh, and let us not forget the time frame. I went back to work in January 2020, right before the pandemic hit. Friend, if I knew then what I know now, I might have stayed at home a little while longer.

During my interview for the new position, I had the opportunity to give a presentation on my background, my leadership style, and my vision for the work. I described my brilliance and told the room full of evaluators, "If this is not what you need, I'm not your candidate." Friend, I needed this job. Our savings were almost dried up, but I was too aware of my brilliance by then to compromise.

In addition to my full-time work, I also became a part-time speaker for a global leadership firm. This allowed me to travel to other universities to facilitate leadership training. I was completely in my element. I loved my work and the people I worked with. Yes, the pandemic caused much heartache and many challenges, but I was ready for it. The work demands were greater, and the pressure increased, but I had changed. I knew the value I brought to the team, and I showed up in my brilliance every day. I was living in my brilliance.

Living in brilliance means you have identified your God-given purpose and you're learning how to walk in it. In this season, you begin taking baby steps to follow your purpose, and as a result, you begin to see your positive impact in the lives of others. Your vision for the life you were created to live becomes clearer, and you experience fulfillment in knowing you are right where you were created to be. People start to recognize your value and call on you for help that aligns with your brilliance. You notice brilliance flowing freely in multiple areas of your life, and you begin to consistently show up in full authenticity without concern for the opinions of others. The goal is to end each day knowing you did exactly what you were created to do. In living in brilliance, you know your impact is divine, and you know where that power comes from.

Brilliance Calls

Edward and I knew in our hearts I wouldn't be in my new AVP position very long, but we had no idea my time there would be as short as it was. In our minds, I'd be in the role for least five years and probably more. We expected I would be there long enough to accomplish major goals for the institution and to build a foundation for the business God had placed in my heart. This dream was alive, and I could no longer ignore it. So I resolved to serve well in my full-time job while building my business after hours. Even in my hiring negotiations, I ensured I'd be supported in working with the leadership firm and accepting invitations to speak for my business as they came my way.

About two years into my new position, I felt transition coming. It felt like emotional and spiritual pressure squeezing me out of my position. I found myself having to sacrifice opportunities to pursue this dream because my full-time job required extensive time and attention. I found myself conflicted between my love for my work and the calling to do more. I found myself losing passion for the work and gaining passion for my next season. I wrestled within myself as I attempted to ignore the sense that transition was on the way. This felt too soon. What would people think? What would they say? What about my students? What about my team? These leaders believed in me when no one else would. I felt like I owed them.

I came to my senses when I remembered my experience from 2019. That burnout experience taught me to never overstay my welcome again. I was not willing to push through until I could no longer take the internal pressure. I would never hold on too long again. I was not willing to burn out again due to disobedience. So I prayed to God, asking Him to speak to my heart. "God, I will trust you better this time. Tell me what you want me to do."

After an especially challenging day at work, my prayer became more specific. "God, I cannot continue to do both. I must be all in at work or all in with this dream. I feel split between two worlds. I can no longer be caught between the two. I will do whatever you tell me to do. If you tell me to stay at work, I will let the dream go until it's time for it. If you tell me to go all in on the dream, I will sacrifice my job. I trust you. Speak, Lord. Your servant is listening."

Well, He didn't take long to speak. The very next day, I received two calls from two different groups of people. One call was an invitation to be the keynote speaker at a regional conference in Texas. The other call was an opportunity to provide leadership training for a healthcare organization in my state. I hadn't pitched myself or requested either invitation. Honestly, for one of them, I had no idea how they'd found me. Each invitation offered my monthly salary as an honorarium for the work. Say. No. More. I went from speaking for free to making my monthly executive salary in one day of work.

More than the money, I had a supernatural peace I hadn't experienced in months. I knew it was time to leap. There was no doubt in my mind that the time had come to go all in. I had a message to share, and people were ready to hear it. Brilliance was calling, and I had to answer.

Pursuit is inevitable after discovering your brilliance. There's no need for overperforming. The holy conflict created in your soul will push you toward brilliance. You must answer the call to remain at peace.

Grief Is Part of the Process

The grieving process began shortly after I received those calls. In August 2021, as we prepared to move the freshmen class of students into the residence halls, I was overcome with grief. I arrived on campus early on the first day of move-in to make sure we were set and ready to welcome our new students and their families. As I pulled into the parking space, an overwhelming grief filled my heart. I wept. All of a sudden, I knew this would be my last freshman move-in. I hadn't told anyone yet, but I knew without a doubt I would never do this work again.

For more than twenty years of my life I'd had some role in welcoming new students to college, and in that moment, I felt that chapter closing. I was wrecked. I didn't weep because I didn't trust God. I didn't weep because I was concerned for my future. I wept because I truly loved the work. I had poured my heart and soul into college students for my entire adult life, and it was time to do something different.

The weeping didn't end with freshman move-in. I cried when I told my boss. Tears fell as I told my team. My voice broke every time

I made the announcement of my resignation to a group of students. I wept on my last day as I facilitated my last commencement ceremony. I wept as I drove away from that event. As excited as I was for my next season, my heart grieved leaving what I'd loved so deeply for so long.

It's one thing to give up something that's hurting you. It's logical to walk out of a bad situation. However, giving up something that seems to be working is a tall order. The salary was good. My team was great. The work was in alignment with my brilliance. It was good enough, but I knew there was more. Purpose will require you to surrender good enough to walk into destiny.

In episode 82 of *Disrupting Burnout*, "Obedience Is the Success," I speak with Shomoneik Brown about her transition from an educator for over eighteen years to working full time at her church. [1] Shomoneik shares how she served at the same school from her internship through all the years of her career. She even had the same classroom she had interned in. God told her 2022 would be her last year teaching, and her heart grieved at the thought of leaving her students and her team. Her heart was broken as she submitted her resignation letter and walked through the process of moving on. However, just as I experienced, after a season of grieving, joy came.

Not only did God allow Shomoneik to use her experience in education to impact His kingdom, but He has honored her secret petition to become a singer by allowing her to minister internationally with Forward City Worship. God will never require you to give something without returning more to you than you gave. Trust Him in the grief. He promised to give joy in exchange for your mourning (Isaiah 61:3).

Friend, allow me to pause for a moment here to let you know you're exactly where you need to be. Grief is a place where all of us think about walking away from brilliance. As the old mindsets are stripped away and you get to the core of your brilliance, you may experience a conflict of the soul. There will be moments when you feel the weight of grief, but at the same time, you know you're going to be okay. You may be weeping and encouraged at the same time. You may feel heavy and have great expectations at the same time. More than one thing can be true, but this season may be confusing if you're not clear about what's happening. Surrender to the grief. Your brilliance is going to shine forth like never before.

Close your eyes and see yourself busting through the old season and emerging into new light. Your life will never be the same. That can be scary and exciting. Allow yourself to hold space for both emotions. You know too much now to remain in a stuck place. You've been exposed to too much. You know too much about you now. You know too much about your purpose to be satisfied with complacency. Surrender. If you need to cry, cry. If you need to talk, find a good listening ear and talk. Pay a therapist if you need to. There is nothing to accomplish at this moment. There's no action step except to surrender. You are in a beautiful place. Find the beauty through the grief.

Disappointing Your People

In my journey through brilliance, I've had opportunities to practice disappointing people. Although this is still a growth area for me, I understand it's necessary to choose brilliance over the desires of others. This includes people I love deeply. Every yes to God caused me to disappoint someone I care about. Pursuing the will of God caused me to leave family and my hometown to move halfway across the country. I'm not as accessible to people as they would like me to be now that I'm so focused on my brilliance. Leaving a job disappointed my leadership, staff, and students. Moving to a new city disappointed loved ones and community members. Resigning from a ministry assignment disappointed church leadership and the people I ministered to through that ministry.

I discovered, at one point, my primary obstacle to obeying God quickly and completely was people pleasing. It breaks my heart when I feel I'm disappointing someone. However, choosing the desires of another person over God's desires for me is idolatry, and I will not bow to idols. I have tasted and seen that living in brilliance is worth the sacrifice. I have also experienced how people who love me adjust to support me and those who are not meant to continue the journey with me eventually fall away. Trust God enough to obey Him in your steps through brilliance even when your people don't understand. Give Him your heart and He will protect your reputation.

Rest and Pursue

Pursuing brilliance does not mean hustling or grinding. God does not need you to create brilliance. He is the Creator; He just needs you to agree with His thoughts about you. In pursuit of brilliance, you will remain at peace. You will remain at rest. Pursue means to take the steps ordered for you by the Lord (Psalm 37:23-24). Pursue means to hear God's instructions for your brilliance and take steps of faith as He leads you. You do not have to fight to be seen or recognized. Forget the algorithms of social media or trying to impress people.

I used to struggle with what it means to rest and work. This concept felt like an unsolvable contradiction. I learned to rest and work means to follow God's instructions from a place of peace. Do not get ahead of Him and do not fall into striving. Trust He has everything you need planned out even when you cannot see it. Rest in Him and walk with Him. God will bring you into your land of plenty, and everything you need will be there upon arrival. Your only work is to obey His instructions, step by step.

Edward was the first person I told when I knew it was time for me to transition out of the AVP role. He wasn't trying to hear it at first. He thought my ambition was getting the best of me. This announcement didn't fit the timeline we'd agreed upon, so he dismissed it for a few weeks. He didn't take me seriously until I came home one day and said, "Babe, I wrote my resignation letter today." His response is still hilarious to me today: "Now wait a minute! We need to talk about this."

I hadn't submitted the resignation yet, but I'd felt compelled to write the letter that day. I did not allow myself to become anxious about his response. I was determined not to badger him about my next move. I decided to rest in what God had said. I decided if I had truly heard from God, then God would also tell my husband. And He did.

Edward came to me a few days later with tears in his eyes. He explained how he had been awake most of the night. God had brought his attention to a sermon Edward had written a couple of years earlier but never preached publicly. In the sermon, "Step into the Water," Edward wrote how the children of Israel crossed more than one body of water before walking into their promised land. I've always heard preachers talk about them crossing the Red Sea on dry ground with Pharaoh and the Egyptian army pursuing them from Exodus 14, but in Joshua 3 and 4, we learn they also crossed the Jordan River without drowning. As he read the sermon notes, Edward knew God was saying it was time for us to cross again. He knew it was time for me to transition into full-time entrepreneurship.

After that night, Edward became more convinced than I was. When I told him I wanted to give a couple months' notice, he tried to convince me to give less. He was so sure about what God said he was ready to jump in. Without any pressure from me, God spoke to my husband in a way only He can.

I didn't have a plan for next steps when I submitted my letter of resignation. I just knew the Lord said to end this position before the end of the year. I had the two invitations I mentioned earlier to look forward to, but there had to be more to sustain us. Once again, I was leaving a six-figure salary to walk into the unknown. At least I'd give notice this time.

I prayed about when I should submit the letter to my supervisor, and I honored the instruction I heard. I fumbled through the conversation with her because I honestly didn't know what to say. Normally, we would tell the person our reasons for leaving and what we plan to do next. Well, I didn't have a plan to share, and I wasn't sure she would understand "God told me to."

God provided even in that moment. As I fumbled through my explanation, we were interrupted by a medical emergency on campus. We immediately left that conversation to support the emergency efforts. Everything ended up okay on campus, and I didn't have to continue rambling. Praise the Lord!

One week later, I got a call from an organization I was familiar with. (I wasn't sure how they knew I had resigned since the email notification to my campus had just been sent.) In short, that organization brought me on to serve them for the first seven months of the next year. After obeying God to submit my resignation, I went from no plan to securing a seven-month contract within a matter of one week. God provides for brilliance.

God does not need your hustle. He just desires your obedience.

Tim Ross, @upsetthegram on Instagram, former pastor of Embassy City Church and creator and host of the podcast *The Basement with Tim Ross*, transitioned from lead pastor to podcast host in 2022. On several episodes of his podcast, Tim shares how God instructed him to release his role as lead pastor of the church he founded after seven years of pastoring and to transition the church to a young minister, Tim Rivers. Tim Ross told how this call to transition felt sudden and out of timing, but he and his wife, Juliette, obeyed the voice of the Lord.

In his sermon "Qualified to Multiply,"[2] Tim declared the church has grown exponentially with Tim Rivers in leadership. He also shared how God led him to podcasting, an area in which he had no experience. At the time of this writing, *The Basement* has over 225,000 subscribers on YouTube after only a few months of existence. This number does not account for the tens of thousands of audio downloads.

On April 3, 2023, Hector Guerrero, @hectoralexguerrero on Instagram and the podcast manager for *The Basement with Tim Ross*, posted: "No Marketing, No Strategy, No Overachieving in posting. The power in dialogue, organic 'word of mouth' sharing, and God being in the algorithm has been the game changer for us." Tim Ross went from reaching hundreds within his church walls to reaching hundreds of thousands by pursuing his brilliance. He went from a massive travel schedule and juggling pastor responsibilities to podcasting unscripted from his living room.

God took the same brilliance Tim used to pastor, mentor, and coach individuals and couples through his years of ministry and put that brilliance on a platform where Tim is reaching the masses and his family is well cared for with less effort from Tim. God does not need your hustle. He just desires your obedience.

Here's one more example of God's provision in my transition. The piece I grieved most of all was my regular connection to students. I love college students, and I recognize the sacredness of this season in their lives. One of my greatest honors has been walking with them through this special time. Well, God has a way of working all things together for good. During my transition, our pastor spoke with me about creating a campus ministry connected to our church. We launched that ministry two months after my last day on the job.

God returned to me the part of the job I would miss the most. He proved I don't need a special title or specific job to minister to college students. My job was just one avenue, but God proved He has many avenues for brilliance to flourish.

Rest. He's got this!

Rest. It will be better than you can ask, think, or imagine.

Rest. He does not miss any detail.

Rest. The Father loves you and knows what you need.

Rest. He created you for the brilliance and the brilliance for you.

Rest and live in brilliance.

A Lifestyle of Release

Get used to living with your hands open. Living in brilliance means trusting God enough for Him to give and take away as He sees fit. I assumed my sacrificing season was over after walking away from my twenty-year career due to burnout and later giving up another six-figure salary when I transitioned out of the AVP role. I just knew I had passed the sacrifice test in heaven. I was wrong. There was more to release.

During my five months out of work in 2019, I got an opportunity to work with the wonderful international leadership training firm I mentioned earlier. At first, I loved the work because it was so aligned with my passions for speaking and training. It was also helpful that the stipends assisted in our financial recovery when we needed it the most. In fall 2022, however, I began to feel differently about this work. Although I love the work and the people connected to this agency something about this particular assignment just did not feel right anymore. It's interesting how something that was the answer to prayer in one season can be the thing that holds you back in a different season. I didn't understand why I was feeling this way, but I couldn't ignore it.

In prayer, I asked God what He was trying to tell me. He clearly said I was to release this assignment. I was heartbroken at the thought of losing these people, these opportunities, and honestly, this income, but I knew what He'd said. I was in the middle of projects and felt my professionalism would be questioned again, but God had spoken. I must admit I was very reluctant and held on much longer than I should have, but eventually I told my dear friend who'd brought me into the company that I needed to step away from the work. They replaced me in my projects pretty quickly, but they didn't understand why I needed to let go.

People will not always understand what God has told you to do. His instructions rarely align with human culture or wisdom. Trust Him. He is aware of your needs and will meet them in His own way.

I had more letting go to do. Remember how kind God was when He allowed Edward and me to launch a college ministry so I could remain connected to college students? Yep, I had to give that up too. He allowed us to walk with those young adults for about a year and a half, building a foundation for the ministry, and then He released us from those responsibilities. We both prayed and fasted, and we felt strongly we needed to get out of the way so the ministry could go to the next level. We were even more secure after the peace we experienced when we told our pastor and the young adults we worked with. This transition was not without tears. It broke my heart to release them, but if I've learned anything about God, I know His will is perfect.

The call to release does not mean you got it wrong. When I felt the call to release my AVP position after only two years, I wondered if I'd made the wrong decision in taking the job in the first place. I wondered if this new call to leave the university was a correction because I had missed God's original instruction. Now, I can see I heard correctly both times. It was a call of brilliance for me to take that job in January 2020 as the pandemic loomed in our future. My specific brilliance in crisis management was needed in that place as we cared for our students, navigated changing mandates, and held space for fear and uncertainty. It was also no coincidence that as the university transitioned into a new sense of normal, God sent me to my next crisis assignment to coach and support professional women through burnout.

Something that was right for you in one season may be wrong for you now. You didn't get it wrong; you are just being called to transition. Living in brilliance requires a constant willingness to release and respond to the new call. You can trust His plan and surrender to the transition.

More than any accomplishment I've ever enjoyed, sacrificing back to God the gifts He has given me and watching how He responds has created the most powerful and precious moments of my life. I am convinced this book would not have been written if I hadn't obeyed God's instruction to release the leadership company and the college ministry. Not only did my schedule open for writing time, but my mind and heart opened to hear what He would have me share with you here. I had more space to spend time with Him to see what He would say to us here.

God will never require something from us that He does not multiply and return in the most beautiful way. Luke 6:38 says, "Give, and you will receive. Your gift will return to you in full—pressed down, shaken together to make room for more, running over, and poured into your lap. The amount you give will determine the amount you get back." In church, we often use this scripture to talk about money, but really, Christ was encouraging us to be compassionate and forgiving, avoiding judgment, because whatever you give to others will overflow back to you. In the same way, whatever you give to God will return to you in full and overflowing. You can trust Him. If we, as faulty human beings, know how to care well for our children, how much more can we trust our Heavenly Father to give us what we need when we need it (Matthew 7:11).

Stir Up the Gift

Live in brilliance by fanning the flames of your passions. Paul begins his second letter to Timothy in the New Testament with an exhortation and instruction (2 Timothy 1). Paul applauds Timothy for his great faith. It's the same faith Paul saw in Timothy's grandmother, Lois, and his mother, Eunice. Paul acknowledges Timothy's powerful legacy as well as his own fortitude in faith. And as a result of this great faith Paul instructs Timothy "to fan into flames the spiritual gift God gave you when I laid my hands on you" (2 Timothy 1:6). You may be more familiar with the language of the King James Version of the Bible which says to "stir up the gift of God." Paul acknowledged Timothy had a gift and helped him understand that gift needs to be stirred and stoked like a fire to thrive.

Often, 2 Timothy 1:6 is quoted alone, but it makes so much more sense in context. After telling Timothy to stir up the gift, Paul admonishes him: "For God has not given us a spirit of fear and timidity, but of power, love, and self-discipline" (2 Timothy 1:7). Paul never said fear is not real. He also did not say fear is a sin. Paul didn't pretend Timothy wouldn't experience fear as He obeyed God in his brilliance. This was just a reminder that fear of stepping out into brilliance does not come from God. Honor the emotion, but do not allow fear to determine your action.

Our Heavenly Father does not give us fear, and I don't know about you, but if He didn't give it to me, I don't want it! Instead of fear, our God gives us power, love, and self-discipline. These are the spiritual ingredients to your brilliance.

The word power in this verse, in the original Greek language of the New Testament, is the word *dynamis*, pronounced doo-nam-is. [3] It is the root word for our English term "dynamite."

Dynamis means the following:[3]

- strength, power, ability
- inherent power, power residing in a thing by virtue of its nature, or which a person or thing exerts and puts forth
- power for performing miracles
- moral power and excellence of soul
- the power and influence that comes from riches and wealth
- power and resources arising from numbers
- power consisting of or resting upon armies, forces, hosts

Synonyms of *dynamis* include force, effectiveness, might, and natural ability.[3] Friend, do you realize how powerful you are? You can change the entire course of a meeting, interaction, negotiation, agreement, crisis, or conversation just by showing up in your brilliance. There is an explosion of power when you live in brilliance. The power of Holy Spirit shows up when you show up. There is a lasting impact on people when you operate in your brilliance. Whether you are called to the home, church, schools, health care, corporate arena, military, or any other industry, you should leave a powerfully positive impression everywhere you go. People should feel something after encountering you. They may not know what to call it, but they will know something special occurred in and around them when you were in the room.

> *Brilliance is going to cost you something, and love is the account you draw from to pay the cost.*

Love is the fountain from which your brilliance flows. Living in your brilliance is not always convenient or comfortable. There will be many days when you don't feel adequate or compelled to show up. Love causes us to serve when we ourselves need to be served. Love for God and love for His people keep us actively living in our brilliance. Even in brilliance, there will be moments when you just don't want to do whatever you need to do. You show up because of love. You serve because of love. You minister because of love. Love does not mean you overwork or return to overwhelm, but it does mean you do the thing that brings glory to God.

Brilliance is going to cost you something, and love is the account you draw from to pay the cost. God taught us to keep love first as He sacrificed His first and only begotten son so we may return to the right relationship with Him (John 3:16). He loved first; therefore, we love. 1 Corinthians 13:13 reminds us: "Three things will last forever—faith, hope, and love—and the greatest of these is love."

I love the way the Amplified version of the Bible defines self-discipline. The Amplified translation of the Bible shares 2 Timothy 1:7 in this way:

> For God did not give us a spirit of timidity or cowardice or fear, but [He has given us a spirit] of power and of love and of sound judgment and personal discipline [abilities that result in a calm, well-balanced mind and self-control].

This verse gives a clear picture of God's expectation for the state of our souls—calm, well-balanced, and controlled. Culture has created an idol of purpose that tells us we must be "booked and busy" and #teamnosleep. That is not brilliance, Friend. That life is reckless and out of order. Our Heavenly Father calls us to calm, a well-balanced mind, and self-control. Here's the good news, you don't have to achieve this alone. God gives us what we need to live in this state of calm and discipline. Our job is to fall more deeply in love with Him so His characteristics shine through our lives. Brilliance is not "booked and busy." Brilliance is not constantly chasing the next thing. Your brilliance is full of power, love, and self-discipline.

Positioned to Obey

Obedience is the primary thing and you must be positioned to obey. You cannot obey God if you cannot hear Him. You cannot hear Him if you are not in relationship with Him. Please allow me to offer a word for those who may struggle to hear God's voice.

First, do not struggle. God wants you to hear Him, so you don't have to strive or fight. He desires you to walk with Him, daily, just as the disciples walked with Jesus. The way to develop such a relationship with the Father is through spiritual disciplines—practices, relationships, and experiences that lead to us encountering God and growing in Him. Adele Ahlberg Calhoun, author of *Spiritual Disciplines Handbook*, says spiritual disciplines give us space in our lives to spend time with our Savior.[4] Spiritual disciplines include prayer, gratitude, worship, giving, serving, fasting, and studying the Word of God to name a few.

Do not be overwhelmed by that list. Start small. God is patient. He is not impressed by piety. He just desires your love. The cool thing about spiritual disciplines is the more you practice, the more you crave.

At one time, I couldn't stay awake to say a decent prayer. Now, I pray all day long through my devotion time, breath prayer, and prayer walks. At one point in my life, scripture was confusing and boring to me. Now, I consume it like soul food. This maturity didn't come because I'm so good. My hunger for Him grew because as I took steps toward Him, He took steps toward me. Now, I cannot get enough! "You're blessed when you've worked up a good appetite for God. He's food and drink in the best meal you'll ever eat" (Matthew 5:6 [MSG]).

God meets you at your desire. As a matter of fact, the urging you have to be closer to Him is proof that God is working in your heart. "You wouldn't want more of God if the Holy Spirit wasn't first seeking you."[4] For a comprehensive resource on spiritual disciplines, refer to *Spiritual Disciplines Handbook: Practices that Transform Us*, by Adele Ahlberg Calhoun.[4]

The foundation of living in brilliance is obedience to the God who made you. He crafted you specifically for the life he called you to live and the only way to achieve that life is through your daily journey with Him. Fighting, striving, and hustling lead us to the throes of burnout. Obedience releases us to live fully in brilliance.

Do the HeartWork

Write the vision. What do you think about when you imagine your perfect life? If money and time were not an issue, and you were living one hundred percent in God's will for your life, what would that look like? Write the vision and "give God something to bless," as my coach Patrice Cunningham Washington often says.[5]

Download the *Disrupting Burnout* journal for a fillable copy of this activity at patricebuckner jackson.com/journal or scan the QR code for access.

Write your vision following these guidelines:

- Release the pressure of whether it's realistic or not. Allow yourself to dream without restriction.
- Describe the vision in detail.
- Do not leave anything out.
- Include all aspects of your life.
- Do not judge your thoughts or wonder how it will happen. Write it all.

Here are some prompts to help you get started writing your vision:

- Describe your ideal week.
- What does your life outside of work look like?
- Where do you live?
- What excites you about your work?
- Who do you serve?
- What impact are you having on their lives?
- How are you sharing your God-given gifts with the world?

Chapter 12

Evidence of Brilliance

I am so proud of my clients who are doing their HeartWork. I have the privilege of walking with phenomenal women (and a few brilliant men) from all over the country who are dedicated to this journey. They are checking their baggage, building powerful boundaries, and not just discovering, but maximizing their innate, unique brilliance. Here are a few of their stories.

Jill was a participant in a business coaching program where I was invited to serve as the mindset coach. At the end of that program, Jill reached out to learn how we could continue working together. She explained how she had endured many transitions in her life and was facing another crossroads. Jill had been out of corporate America for a while and needed to decide if she should return to the office or continue pursuing entrepreneurship. While she had many marketable skills, drawn by a new church, she felt called to make a long-distance move to restart in a new state.

Instead of focusing directly on the choices before her, Jill and I dug into the HeartWork strategies. I knew if she could clear some clutter, her next step would be undeniable. In the process, Jill became more aware of her unique brilliance and took steps to transition to her new state.

About this experience, Jill said:

> I heard "HeartWork," and that's when I realized I needed to do the "hard work." Avoiding the hard work kept me stuck for years. I learned true transformation requires work, not works (performance). It's the inside job that had me looking at what was in my "backpack." I started a journey to healing and wholeness I never thought I needed.

Jill now lives in her new state, has just purchased a beautiful new home, and has opened that home to support other women in pursuing their God-given purpose. When I first met Jill, she would rarely unmute her camera for fear of being seen. Now she is one of the first to speak up in our HeartWork Community.

Tina is an accomplished professor who found herself frustrated by the culture and politics of the academy. When I met Tina, she had recently published her first book, was raising a toddler, and was preparing to move her family to a new state. Tina was wrestling with whether she wanted to remain in academia or if it was time to do something different. She had toiled to gain respect in her field, and it seemed the finish line was constantly moving.

Through the HeartWork strategies, Tina established new boundaries and accepted permission to manage her own energy regardless of imposed cultural norms. She also discovered a hidden passion for mentoring Black graduate students through their graduate experience and into their career field. In our work together, Tina recognized her greatest professional joy had been supporting Black students during this phase of their education, and she found she was already doing this work with several personal mentees but had never acknowledged it as an expression of her brilliance.

Tina created a vision for a retreat she will facilitate to serve these students, and she gained new clarity concerning her career path. In her own words, "I went into each session knowing that I wouldn't be able to hide or play small, and I left each session crystal clear about next steps I could take to move closer to my goals. This was truly a transformational experience."

I met Amy during a workshop for professional women. She approached me in tears after the session and shared how my burnout story was so closely connected to her story. She had walked away from a long career in dentistry and shifted into real estate, where she could set her own hours while she raised her babies. Amy now found herself in a searching place. She wasn't sure if she'd ever found her unique, innate brilliance, and she had a strong desire to know exactly what God required from her so she could obey.

Within the HeartWork Community, Amy found much more than a career path. She found community and rest for her soul. She discovered she had been toiling and striving to obtain God's favor when He desired her to learn the "unforced rhythms of grace" (Matthew 11:29 [MSG]). Through our walk together, Amy discovered several options for her next career steps, and she is learning to surrender to her current season as God continues to reveal next steps.

In her own words, Amy shared:

> When I met Dr. PBJ at a professional women's workshop, I was immediately drawn to her and recognized something different about her. She had so much energy, and I was stuck in this place of always trying to do the thing God called me to do. Dr. PBJ helped me to shift my mindset from being consumed with wanting to do the things that God called me to do instead of being who God created me to be. And I've learned that when I focus on that, the doing comes organically. In the Discover Your Brilliance group, Dr. PBJ has taught me how to, and that it's okay to, tap into the innate abilities God designed within me. I learned that it's ok to give myself permission to dream again . . . Kingdom-size dreams.

Ramona is a multi-passionate woman dividing her time as an educator, a speaker, a minister, a singer, and a conference host, and she takes on renovation projects with her husband in her limited spare time. Ramona came to our coaching community with an urge to leave education so she could fully pursue speaking and conference hosting. Although she was ready to get out of the classroom, she felt a definitive instruction that it was not her time to go. Prompted by Holy Spirit, she had recently begun a graduate degree.

Ramona discovered there was a bridge set before her. She realized her degree and all her experience were setting her up to transition out of the classroom and into education leadership. She saw how God had set a path before her to become an administrator in education, which confirmed her urge to leave the classroom and provided a bridge to full-time ministry sometime in the future.

Ramona settled into her steps of obedience and anticipates taking every step with God.

Ramona shared:

> The one thing I've learned while being in the Discover Your Brilliance community is to own my confidence as I grow in my brilliance. My brilliance is using my voice to lead. The most impactful moment for me, shared on the weekly Discover Your Brilliance platform, was to be intentional about my rest because candid conversations about self-care were necessary for my growth. Dr. Patrice Buckner Jackson is a midwife to the women desiring more than a burnout testimony! My brilliance birthing experience will be a legacy to remember. Thank you, Dr. PBJ, for creating a safe incubator for me and other women to be nurtured and embrace their authenticity in self-discovery!

Kris is a dedicated HeartWorker from my first podcast episode to every program I have opened. She was the first person to make a comment on one of my videos and provided the first testimonial I received by email. She's a woman who has cared for people for her entire adult life, and the message of disrupting burnout resonates with her heart.

When Kris came to the HeartWork Community, she was facing the "empty nest" season of her life. She had given everything to raise her children, and now that they were moving on, she didn't know who she was anymore. She had an undeniable desire to take a bold step just for herself, but she didn't know what that step should be. Kris found herself battling depressive symptoms as she grappled with her own significance without her children.

Through the HeartWork Community, Kris sought counseling for the first time and began to set boundaries with her husband, adult children, other people, and her job. She also gained a new understanding of her own gifts. Kris began to see how she had always been on the front lines to support people who were having a bad day. From working in a mental health facility to her job at a university and supporting her elderly mother-in-law, Kris is the problem-solver you want to meet when your day seems to be falling apart. She's now in the process of understanding this brilliance and seeking God on how He might use her gift in this new season of her life.

In her own words, Kris shared, "Dr. PBJ welcomed us with patience and always reminded us that we have all that we need in us. We just have to see it for ourselves. She takes you on a journey from just being to becoming. My life is forever changed. Her faith and wisdom will remind you that with God, all things are possible!"

None of these women have completed their HeartWork journey because there is no finish line. You will continue this journey as long as there is breath in your body. There is no need to go back to the Cycle of Burnout, but as you grow in brilliance, you'll transition to new levels. New levels require a freshly checked backpack, adjusted boundaries, and a new awareness of who you are becoming.

The HeartWork strategies bring powerful revolution and revival to women like you. By checking your baggage, you uncover belief systems that hold you back from God's plan for your life. In building boundaries, you protect your brilliance and everything that means most to you. And through discovering your brilliance, you reclaim the life God created you to live and make an undeniable impact on the world around you. In this journey, you bring glory to God and invite His goodness into your life by learning to live by the specific pattern He set for you.

You are uniquely and wonderfully made.

> "Thank you for making me so wonderfully complex! Your workmanship is marvelous—how well I know it" (Psalm 139:14).

You are a masterpiece.

> "For we are God's masterpiece. He has created us anew in Christ Jesus, so we can do the good things he planned for us long ago" (Ephesians 2:10).

There is no one else like you, Friend. Your brilliance is needed on the earth. No one else can do the work assigned to your hands. And the best news? You will never have to do it alone; God carries the full weight of the outcome, and He sends people to yoke up with you to get it all done. The weight of your brilliance is easy and light. Anything else is unacceptable.

Discover your brilliance. Pursue that brilliance and let it shine. Hiding your brilliance kept you chained to the Cycle of Burnout. No more retreating. It's time for you to be everything God created you to be. Now you have the strategies. It's time to shine!

I will close our time here together as I close every podcast episode.

> As always, Friend,
> You are powerful, you are significant, and you are loved.
> Love always,
> PBJ

Do the HeartWork

Write your brilliance story.

- What have you discovered about your brilliance through the HeartWork journey?
- What is your innate, unique brilliance?
- What evidence have you discovered to support your brilliance?
- How will you pursue your brilliance?

Share your story with me. Email me at info@educarestrategies.com or scan the code below.

Acknowledgements

Thank you, Father! I thought this work was for them, but through this writing, you showed me a new revelation of your love for me. Your love never fails, and I'm grateful to be a daughter of the King.

Edward, you've been there for every valley and every mountaintop since the first day we said hello. Thank you for holding me up when I could not stand. #stillworththewait

To my BabyGirl. You are everything I ever dreamed of. Your wisdom is beyond your years, and you make me proud every day. Thank you for making me Mama Patrice. Thank you for loving me. Thank you for allowing me to love you.

In loving memory of Granma Ozella and Grandaddy Bill. Your legacy is love. You always made me feel like the most loved little girl in the whole wide world, and you shared that same love with everyone around you. Now it's my turn to pass it on. I'll love you forever. I'll take it from here.

Mama, *thank you*. I cannot imagine how afraid you must have been at sixteen years old, but I do know the strength and courage you proved by deciding my life was worth it. Thank you for making us pray before school every day. Thank you for making me teach Sunday School, starting at age ten. You had us at Sunday School every Sunday morning even if we were the only people there. I did not understand why you would make me "teach" when there was no audience to learn. I did not understand why you sometimes made me teach the adult lesson. I know now you were stirring up this gift. Thank you for allowing Holy Spirit to guide you in raising us. You can tell a tree by the fruit it bears. This is your harvest, Mama, because you sowed for this. All of us rise up and call you BLESSED. I love you.

To my Daddy(s). God knew exactly who I needed and when I needed them to become everything He created me to be. Thank you for everything you invested in me.

Kimmie, Jr, Tiff, Que, Lamont, and Malia, being your big sister is one of my greatest joys. I love each of you and I am so proud to be your sister.

To my nieces and nephews. You are the most beautiful and brilliant nieces and nephews in the whole world. There is no good thing that is off limits to you. Dream BIG and go after it all. Because of the God you believe in, *you cannot lose*! Auntie Trice loves you!

Candice L. Davis, my book coach, thank you for fueling my belief and equipping me for this work. Thank you for teaching me how to accomplish this goal. You are masterful in your work, and the evidence is all the authors you have supported through publication. It is an honor for me to be among the ranks trained by you.

Patrice Cunningham Washington, my purpose midwife, thank you for seeing the brilliance in me and not allowing me to continue to shrink. Thank you for keeping me honest and encouraged as I continue to pursue His path for my life. Your life is a blessing to the earth, and I am eternally grateful that you came into my world. I am forever changed.

Kristell, Tiesha, Raymona, Wendy, Sherie, and Danielle, it is quite a blessing for a person to say they've had one consistent best friend in their lifetime. I am a wealthy woman because God blessed me with all of you. Thank you for your love and grace when I run into isolation. You love even when you do not understand. Thank you for welcoming me back when I am ready to emerge. Thank you for understanding my heart and always cheering me on. You all are jewels, and I am overwhelmed that God would be so good to me.

To Dr. Teri Melton. Thank you for believing when I did not. Thank you for knocking on my front door that evening. Everything I write started the moment you believed in me.

To my students, all of you. You gave me the honor of being a part of your life. There is no greater gift. I'm grateful for it all.

Sharon, Thank you for your Yes! You are an answer to my prayers and I am so glad you decided to "Come on in the Room." I don't know where this journey is taking us, but I'm grateful we get to do this together.

To Anita, Jemekka, Jael, Kristell, and Dr. Raymona. Thank you for sowing your time and love into this work. You created a space where my raw, unedited vulnerability was safe. You sowed honesty and love to sharpen the sword that is this book. Your fingerprints are all over these chapters, and I am grateful.

To my current and future clients. You are brilliant. God made you that way. Before you had any opportunity to perform or achieve, you were already brilliant. End of story.

Notes

Chapter 1: I Was Born for This

1. "Holy," Blue Letter Bible, accessed September 10, 2023, https://www.blueletterbible.org/lexicon/g40/kjv/tr/0-1/
2. Marissa Farrow, *The Amazing Weight: The Gift, Grief, and Glory of the Called* (Towson: Halo Creative Group, 2018), 8-9.

Chapter 3: Disrupting Burnout

1. "Disrupt," Oxford Languages, accessed September 13, 2023, https://www.google.com/search?scaesv=565014946&sxsrf=AB5stBhgGfOzal44_SeItNWjl2cw4jvug:1694610329253&q=disrupt&si=ACFMAn9VODCs-uG4dZ4pWLt0kJLWKgHXyqQLORxsY1yzeqdlv9pQ2npWEoOoPowda56E_2I2_qsgnUriFHUIc6IiNrX3WBh5ow%3D%3D&expnd=1&sa=X&ved=2ahUKEwjqotS106eBAxVkkWoFHbGFByUQ2v4IegQIDRBe&biw=1393&bih=682&dpr=1
2. "Disrupt," Cambridge Dictionary, accessed July 2, 2023, https://dictionary.cambridge.org/us/dictionary/english/disrupt.
3. Stephanie Marken and Sangeeta Agrawal, "K-12 Workers Have the Highest Burnout Rate in the U.S.," *Gallup*, (June 13, 2022). accessed October 3, 2022, https://news.gallup.com/poll/393500/workers-highest-burnout-rate.aspx
4. "HealthWorker Burnout," U.S. Department of Health and Human Services: Office of the U.S. Surgeon General, accessed September 10, 2023, https://www.hhs.gov/surgeongeneral/priorities/health-worker-burnout/index.html#:~:text=In%20what%20ways%20do%20health,among%20patients%2C%20and%20staffing%20shortages.

5. Ashley Abramson, "The Impact of Parental Burnout," *American Psychological Association* 52, no. 7, (October 1, 2021), accessed October 3, 2022, https://www.apa.org/monitor/2021/10/cover-parental-burnout

6. "Caregiver Burnout," Cleveland Clinic, accessed October 3, 2022, https://my.clevelandclinic.org/health/diseases/9225-caregiver-burnout#:~:text=is%20caregiver%20burnout%3F-,Caregiver%20burnout%20is%20a%20state%20of%20physical%2C%20emotional%20and%20mental,are%20able%2C%20physically%20or%20financially.

7. "Burn-out an 'occupational phenomenon': International Classification of Diseases," World Health Organization (WHO), accessed October 3, 2022, https://www.who.int/news/item/28-05-2019-burn-out-an-occupational-phenomenon-international-classification-of-diseases

8. Christina Maslach and Michael Leiter, *The Burnout Challenge: Managing People's Relationships with Their Jobs*, (Harvard University Press, 2022).

9. National Preparedness Goal, *FEMA*, March 21, 2023, https://www.fema.gov/emergency-managers/national-preparedness/goal#:~:text=The%20National%20Preparedness%20Goal%20describes,tied%20to%20a%20capability%20target.

Chapter 4: Living in Alignment

1. "Soul," Blue Letter Bible, accessed on September 10, 2023, https://www.blueletterbible.org/lexicon/h5315/kjv/wlc/0-1/

2. Kobe Campbell, *Why Am I Like This*, (Thomas Nelson,2023), https://kobecampbell.com/

Chapter 5: What Is Your Tell?

1. "Your Life is Speaking to You," Patrice Washington and Natalie Macneil, accessed September 10, 2023, https://www.youtube.com/watch?v=Enr1nvq6HgY&t=1674s.

2. Rebecca Zucker, *How to Deal with Constantly Feeling Overwhelmed*, Harvard Business Review, (October 10, 2019), https://hbr.org/2019/10/how-to-deal-with-constantly-feeling-overwhelmed#:~:text=level%20of%20responsibility.-,The%20cognitive%20impact%20of%20feeling%20perpetually%20overwhelmed%20

can%20range%20from,impaired%20ability%20to%20problem%20 solve.

3. "Will," Merriam-Webster, (2023), https://www.merriam-webster. com/dictionary/will

4. "Breath," Blue Letter Bible, accessed September 10, 2023, https:// www.blueletterbible.org/lexicon/h5397/kjv/wlc/0-1/

Chapter 6: Check Your Baggage

1. "Forgiving my Father," Disrupting Burnout, Dr. Patrice Buckner Jackson, accessed on November 18, 2020, https://www. patricebucknerjackson.com/podcast/episode/4b9dd886/9-forgivin g-my-father

2. "From Daddy's Perspective," Disrupting Burnout, Dr. Patrice Buckner Jackson, accessed on November 25, 2020, https://www. patricebucknerjackson.com/podcast/episode/4aed7e57/10-fro m-daddys-perspective

Chapter 8: Build Your Boundaries

1. Sue and Neil Thompson, The Critically Reflective Practitioner, (Basingstoke: Palgrave Macmillan, 2008).

2. "One Millimeter Movement," Disrupting Burnout, Dr. Patrice Buckner Jackson and Lia Valencia Key, March 29, 2023, https:// www.patricebucknerjackson.com/podcast/episode/7bbcc771/83-on e-millimeter-movement.

3. "Show Yourself Compassion," Disrupting Burnout, Dr. Patrice Buckner Jackson and Gabi Ruth, April 12, 2023, https://www. patricebucknerjackson.com/podcast/episode/7a787135/85-show-you rself-compassion-with-gabi-ruth

Chapter 9: Boundaries That Work

1. Kobe Campbell, *Why Am I Like This*, (Thomas Nelson,2023), 168.

2. "One Millimeter Movement," Disrupting Burnout, Dr. Patrice Buckner Jackson and Lia Valencia Key, March 29, 2023, https:// www.patricebucknerjackson.com/podcast/episode/7bbcc771/83-on e-millimeter-movement.

3. "Heart," Blue Letter Bible, accessed September 10, 2023, https:// www.blueletterbible.org/lexicon/h3820/kjv/wlc/0-1/

4. "Selah," Blue Letter Bible, accessed September 10, 2023, https://www.blueletterbible.org/lexicon/h5542/kjv/wlc/0-1/

5. John Mark Comer, The *Ruthless Elimination of Hurry* (WaterBrook, 2019).

6. Malinda Fuller, *Obedience over Obedience over Hustle: The Surrender of the Striving Heart*, (Shiloh Run Press, 2019).

7. Tamara Schwarting, The Untold Value of a Professional Sabbatical, Forbes, (2017, December 27). https://www.forbes.com/sites/ellevate/2017/12/22/the-untold-value-of-a-professional-sabbatical/

8. Bridget Shulte, *Overwhelmed: How to Work, Love, and Play When No One Has the Time*, (Picador, 2015).

Chapter 10: Discover Your Brilliance

1. "This is Confusing // Stranger Things Part. 2," Dharius Daniels TV, Sunday, April 23, 2023. accessed from https://www.youtube.com/watch?v=lmlEgdYpKt0

2. "Oprah Winfrey on Career, Life, and Leadership," Stanford Graduate School of Business, April 28, 2014, accessed from https://www.youtube.com/watch?v=6DlrqeWrczs

3. Tunde Oyeneyin, *Speak: Find Your Voice, Trust Your Gut, and Get from Where You Are to Where You Want to Be*, (Simon and Schuster Audio, 2022)

4. "Serena Williams's stroke of genius for overall success," Slack, 2019, accessed from https://slack.com/blog/collaboration/serena-williams-stroke-of-genius-for-overall-success

5. "Maine school custodian helps turn chess team into a real-life 'Queen's Gambit," CBS Evening News, Apr 7, 2023. accessed from https://www.youtube.com/watch?v=EsOcrJpNcOU

Chapter 11: Living in Brilliance

1. "Obedience is the Success with Shomoneik Brown," Disrupting Burnout, Dr. Patrice Buckner Jackson and Shomoneik Brown, March 29, 2023, https://www.patricebucknerjackson.com/podcast/episode/7f2d4c63/82-obedience-is-the-success-with-shomoneik-brown.

2. "Qualified to Multiply," Transformation Church, April 2, 2023, accessed from https://www.youtube.com/watch?v=_6S8HVPhpFo

3. "Dynamis," Blue Letter Bible, accessed September 10, 20123, https://www.blueletterbible.org/lexicon/g1411/kjv/tr/0-1/

4. Adele Ahlberg Calhoun, *Spiritual Disciplines Handbook: Practices that Transform Us* (InterVarsity Press, 2015).
5. "Give God Something to Bless," Patrice Washington, accessed September 10, 2023, https://patricewashington.com/livelife/give-god-something-to-bless/.

Printed in the USA
CPSIA information can be obtained
at www.ICGtesting.com
CBHW081303220124
3655CB00008B/428